TALES FROM THE
NEW YORK JETS
SIDELINE

A COLLECTION OF THE GREATEST
JETS STORIES EVER TOLD

MARK CANNIZZARO

SPORTS
PUBLISHING

www.skyhorsepublishing.com

10 9 8 7 6 5 4 3 2 1

Cannizzaro, Mark.
 Tales from the New York Jets sideline : a collection of the greatest Jets stories ever told / Mark Cannizzaro.
    p. cm.
 ISBN 978-1-61321-033-8 (alk. paper)
1. New York Jets (Football team)--Anecdotes. 2. New York Jets (Football
team)--History. I. Title.
 GV956.N37C36 2011
 796.332'64097471--dc23
                            2011018651

Printed in the United States of America

TO MY WIFE, CAROLYN,
FOR PUTTING UP WITH MY NONSENSE.

CONTENTS

INTRODUCTION

IF YOU'VE TAKEN THE TIME and effort to open to this page, chances are you are one of them.

You know who you are. You're a tortured, teased, and tantalized New York Jets fan. You've endured a lifetime of disappointment with only a speckle of joy sprinkled in but not without experiencing a kaleidoscope of emotions.

You've lived through the angst of playoff-less seasons, one after another after another. You've suffered through the stinging disappointment of heartbreaking playoff losses in the very few times your beloved J-E-T-S, Jets, Jets, Jets have actually qualified for postseason play.

You've absorbed the embarrassment of 1-15. You've watched in horror as defensive end Dennis Byrd, one of the more popular players in team history, suffered spinal damage and was paralyzed after—of all things—he collided with one of his own teammates while trying to sack the quarterback.

You've watched in sadness as former general manager Dick Steinberg, always a classy, dignified, good man, succumbed to cancer.

You've watched in amazement while one player, offensive guard Carlton Haselrig, went missing for weeks and the team could not find him.

You've watched with bewilderment as team owner Leon Hess, while vacationing in the Bahamas, decided one winter morning that Rich Kotite was the answer to his team's annual ailments.

You've watched in anger as Bill Parcells, after bringing the troubled franchise to the brink of the Super Bowl, walked away without finishing the job, leaving the organization in a similar condition to the one it was in when he arrived three years earlier as the savior—in a state of disorganization.

Bill Belichick's tenure as the team's head coach, which lasted some 12 hours, followed. And then, after Belichick's stunning and memorable resignation on the very day he was to be named as head coach, Al Groh was soon in control. That, of course, lasted only a year before Groh fled for the security of the college game at his alma mater, Virginia.

Following the death of Hess and the introduction of Woody Johnson as the new owner of the franchise

Jets fans are waiting to celebrate a championship after all of the heartache and close calls they have endured.

came Herman Edwards. And with Edwards, the fiery, motivational machine, arrived new hope for Jets fans.

The Jets made the playoffs in their first two seasons under Edwards, losing a first-round wild-card playoff game at the end of his first season after dramatically propelling themselves into the postseason with a last-second victory on the final game of the regular season and then winning the AFC Eastern Division and winning a playoff game. His third season was a step-back season foiled by the preseason injury of starting quarterback Chad Pennington, the future of the franchise.

Despite having no title to show for his first three seasons, though, Edwards looked to have the team moving in the right direction.

As he's acclimated himself to New York, Edwards, a highly perceptive type, has become well acquainted with the passion of the Jets fan, truly a unique breed.

"They're very passionate," Edwards said. "Historically, the fans of this organization have been very, very supportive of this football team, particularly considering the fact that the team has led somewhat of a nomad life. The franchise started off as the Titans in New York 40-some years ago and then was at Shea Stadium and then was out of Shea and then was playing in the Meadowlands. ... The fans have just kind of followed them along from place to place. The team goes, and there go the fans with them.

"What's unique about it is there are so many people in the past 25 years that have left New York but are still big Jets fans. They're all over the country. Wherever you go, you've got Jet fans. When we're in Miami, almost half the stadium is filled with Jets fans.

"Based on the fact that the team has not won a lot of championships, it makes you wonder why they stay so loyal. With Dallas, for example, there are so many Cowboys fans because they won so many world championships. Well, the Jets haven't won but one. The Jets fans are waiting on their day to come. They're waiting on their day of deliverance."

1

BRUCE COSLET

WHEN THE JETS BROUGHT in Dick Steinberg as general manager and Bruce Coslet as coach, it seemed they were moving into the 20th century after being stuck in the Joe Walton era.

Coslet, however, proved to be too meteoric in his dealings with the team. He, too, came off as a coach who thought he invented the game, often patronizing reporters and chastising them for having no idea what they were talking about.

All the while, though, Coslet failed to win enough games to support his arrogance. In fact, he coached the Jets for four seasons and never produced a single winning year, making the playoffs once with an 8-8 record and quickly bowing out in a wild-card loss to the Oilers in Houston in 1991-1992.

Most telling of Coslet's downfall was his inept offense, which produced only 36 points in the final six games of the 1993 season. Coslet had arrived as a

Bruce Coslet had all the answers for why the Jets couldn't win. In the end, the result was his firing.

supposed offensive guru after having been a successful offensive coordinator with the Cincinnati Bengals.

BRUCE, WHY?

After his third game as an NFL head coach, Bruce Coslet refused to make his way down from his second-floor office to the press room on the first floor for an interview the day after a 30-7 loss to the Buffalo Bills. Instead, he conducted a conference call from his office to the press room.

The entire scene made for a rather humorous moment as nine beat writers hovered around a small speakerbox talking to the head coach who was in his office—no more than a 20-yard field goal away.

The first question, which came from Peter Finney Jr., then the beat writer for *The New York Post*, was: "Bruce, why are you doing this?"

Coslet explained that he was too busy to come downstairs for a press conference, claiming that because the Buffalo game was a Monday night game, he had no time on a Tuesday for a press conference.

"It's because I don't have time to deal with you guys today," Coslet said. "I'm in the middle of a game plan. I got my whole staff in my office, and we're working on New England, our next opponent. We're a day short, that's the reason. Next question."

COSLET UNPLUGGED

One of Bruce Coslet's memorable moments and first of many attempts at media manipulating came when he closed the doors to the press room in his first year and asked everyone to turn off their tape recorders.

The press room at the Jets' facility, Weeb Ewbank Hall, was crowded even though it was about half full. It was completely silent. Coslet, who always looked nervous, stood with a crumpled piece of white notebook paper that he always had with him. It was his agenda for the day.

Speaking about quarterback Ken O'Brien, whom he inherited upon taking the Jets' job and with whom he wasn't enamored, Coslet went off in an off-the-record session with reporters, "Look, you know my quarterback sucks. I know my quarterback sucks. Everyone knows my quarterback sucks."

Coslet's message: He didn't have the kind of quarterback he needed to win.

"AM I GOING TO BE PARALYZED?"

On November 29, 1992, against Kansas City, Scott Mersereau lined up on defense as he always did. As the play broke, he realized it was a stunt. He ran around the corner and zeroed in on Kansas City quarterback Dave Krieg. Krieg was his for the taking. He ran at him with all of his momentum and strength as Krieg stepped up to throw. POW! Out of nowhere, a helmet hit him in the chest, and he crumpled to the ground, gasping for air.

But Mersereau was lucky. Dennis Byrd, another Jet, had come around the opposite side of the line and grabbed Krieg right as Mersereau got to the quarterback. The helmet that knocked the wind out of Mersereau was Byrd's. Byrd lay motionless on the Giants Stadium turf.

"Am I going to be paralyzed?" he asked as he looked up at the team of Jets doctors.

As Mersereau walked off the field trying to regroup from the blow, he saw Byrd being carried away on a stretcher with the team orthopedist and assistant trainer and realized what had happened and how serious the injury was.

As Byrd was carted away, several teammates hurried over and gently touched him. Veterans James Hasty, Paul Frase, Brian Washington, Mike Brim, R.J. Kors, and

Marvin Washington, his best friend on the team, were among them.

"You know it could happen to you," Jets linebacker Mo Lewis said. "But when it happens to a teammate, it's even more scary because it could've been you."

By the time Byrd was rushed to New York's Lenox Hill Hospital, he had no use of his legs and only partial use of his arms.

WIN ONE FOR BYRD

The week after Dennis Byrd was paralyzed, the Jets faced the Bills in Buffalo. The Bills had beaten the Jets in the teams' previous 10 meetings.

The team's spirits were buoyed by the news that Byrd had gained some voluntary movement in his legs. Before the game, Jets cornerback James Hasty walked up to linebacker Kyle Clifton during pregame warmups. The mood was somber but hopeful, thanks to the news about Byrd. But the pregame feeling was far away from the jacked-up mood the team usually is in as it readies for Sunday battle. Byrd's injury the week before had cast a pall over the team.

"It is in God's plan for us to win," Hasty said to Clifton. "No matter what they do, we are going to win [this] game."

Clifton, one of the most religious men on the Jets' roster at the time, quietly nodded to Hasty, as if to acknowledge that he was on the same wavelength as his teammate and that there was no way he was going to let the team down on that day. Shortly after Hasty's

poignant words to Clifton, the team got together for the pregame huddle and that somber mood took a palpable turn toward raging fire. It was that fire that carried the Jets that day.

Byrd, who'd undergone surgery five days before the game, watched from his hospital room with his wife, Angela, and his parents.

"It was nothing but heart," defensive tackle Mario Johnson said, pointing to his chest. "You tried to keep your emotions in control, but we were all whacked out. I knew Dennis was watching, and I knew if I messed up, I couldn't live with myself, and I knew Dennis couldn't live with it. I was out there playing for Dennis."

The Jets upset the Bills in Buffalo 24-17 in honor of their fallen teammate. It was just one win in a 4-12 season, but it was memorable.

VICTORY CIRCLE

After the victory over the Bills, about 20 Jets players and coaches squeezed into a room adjacent to the visitors' locker room to speak to Dennis Byrd in a telephone conference call. The room was sweaty and cramped. Some players still had full uniforms on. Some were in a state of undress. Nearly all had tears in their eyes.

Cornerback James Hasty told Byrd how fired up the team was in his honor, adding how sad it was that he

Dennis Byrd stands strong during a halftime ceremony at the 1993 season opener—less than a year after this he was paralyzed in a collision with teammate Scott Mersereau.

wasn't there with them to share the moment. Byrd was there, though. It was as if he could reach through that phone line and slap every one his beloved teammates on the back of their helmets to congratulate them. Byrd didn't make any tackles or sacks in that game, but he was the most valuable player in the game, even if from afar.

In fact, Byrd told his teammates that he was, indeed, there with them, causing an uproarious reaction. The mood of the call shifted from tense to celebratory as the players were touched by Byrd's brave candor.

"I have to believe that Dennis' spirit was here, but it wasn't the same as him being physically here," Hasty said. "Dennis was really happy for us. You couldn't ask for a better situation than what happened today."

Defensive end Paul Frase said he thought about Byrd throughout the game, adding, "Whenever I thought about him, I lifted Dennis up to God. I pray for him, and I pray for God to touch his body and touch him with a miracle."

Byrd would slowly recover to the point where he was able to walk again. He went back home to Oklahoma with his family.

TOO MUCH TALK

One day during the 1993 season, Bruce Coslet told reporters early in the day during his daily press conference that he didn't think the Jets had enough talent to make a legitimate run for the playoffs and beyond, clearly indicating that he was doing everything he could with a short deck of cards.

"We just don't have what it takes," he said matter-of-factly.

Reporters quickly went to some of the veteran players and relayed Coslet's words. Some players were infuriated. Team leader Jeff Lageman, a defensive end, particularly took umbrage. He refused to believe his coach would say that with so much of the season still to play. Lageman, usually a player with a good relationship with the press, actually grew angry at the thought and immediately sought out Coslet to confirm his words.

Once player reaction reached Coslet, he realized that he had made a dire mistake.

Later in the day, realizing that he'd clearly put the onus on general manager Dick Steinberg and was sending a bad message to his players, Coslet went into damage control. He made an unusual early-evening trip to the press room at Weeb Ewbank Hall.

Coslet entered, looking frazzled, with a cigarette smoked to its filter and burning its way nearly to his fingers. He stood at the door pleading with reporters not to print his words from earlier in the day.

"Guys, I think you might be misinterpreting what I said earlier today, and I'd really appreciate it if you would not use those quotes," Coslet said, almost begging.

Coslet explained that he was under immense pressure, and he unknowingly let on that Rob Moore, the team's best receiver and offensive threat, wasn't going to be able to play that Sunday with a bad leg injury. He said his words were not meant to tweak Steinberg and pleaded that the stories not be written the way he had stated things earlier.

Reporters were completely taken aback. They went with the original story anyway, which obviously angered not only Coslet but Steinberg.

TALKIN' TRASH

After a 28-7 loss to the Dallas Cowboys, Bruce Coslet got into it with head coach Jimmy Johnson, whom he ripped for continuing to let his defenders blitz in a game that was seemingly already decided. On the way off the field, Coslet berated Johnson for blitzing quarterback Boomer Esiason and knocking him out of the game during garbage time in the fourth quarter. Johnson completely ignored Coslet's rants and walked away.

"I was a little perturbed he would double-safety blitz leading 28-7 and try to knock Boomer out of the game," Coslet said after the game. "I didn't mind him blitzing Browning [Nagle, the backup] when we were down there trying to score. But 28-7? You don't do that."

Johnson was typically smug in his retort.

"Someone needs to pass me a note or give me the rule when we are supposed to blitz and when we can't blitz. I don't know. We just try to win ballgames. When the other team tries to score, we try to stop them. Again, I haven't read the manual yet as far as what defenses we're supposed to play at the end of the game."

CARY ON

One week after the loss to the Cowboys, the Jets traveled to cold Buffalo to face off against the hated Bills.

With 53 seconds left in the game, Cary Blanchard stood behind the 42-yard line and looked at the uprights. The score was 16-14 Buffalo, and this kick would determine whether the Jets went home with a playoff berth or just went home.

Before the game Blanchard had been a perfect 12 for 12 from inside the 40-yard line, but two earlier misses from 27 and 41 yards out had put the pressure on this kick. It was all or nothing.

It turned out to be nothing.

Blanchard reached back and let the ball have it. It looked true and dead straight on.

Then it veered left, as had his other two misses.

"I'm not going to blame anything on the wind," Blanchard said of the nine-degree temperatures with 28-below-zero wind-chill temperatures. "The guys went out there and busted their butts, doing everything they can to get back with a win, which we needed badly. It's disappointing for me to miss three in a game. I don't think I've ever done that in my whole career."

Blanchard was stand-up afterward. And his teammates didn't blame him for the loss.

"He had an off day, but we all do, don't we?" safety Brian Washington said. "He's human."

Still, though, there was a foul feeling of doom amongst the Jets, who'd seen this type of team failure too often before.

"I've been here for four years, and I'm tired of ifs, and I'm tired of almosts. Almost doesn't put a victory in that left-hand win column," Washington said.

"We're missing something. Whatever it is, I don't know," Boomer Esiason said. "If you want to get to that next level, these are the games you have to win."

Under Coslet, the Jets would never get to that next level.

HOUSTON, WE HAVE A PROBLEM

Houston is a place whose mention brings immediate heartburn to Jets fans.

During a familiar stretch of futility, the Jets lost to the Oilers in Houston three years in a row at the end of the season, each loss spinning a different sordid storyline.

On January 2, 1994, the final day of the 1993 season with a playoff berth on the line, the Jets were shellacked 24-0 by a dysfunctional Oilers team, which saw two assistant coaches (Buddy Ryan and Kevin Gilbride) fight with each other on the sideline during the game in the Astrodome.

Making matters so typical of the Jets was the fact that every star aligned perfectly earlier that day to allow them to win and make the playoffs. Before the Jets took the field at the Astrodome in a late game, the Miami Dolphins had lost to the New England Patriots in overtime. That left open the final playoff berth in the AFC for the Jets to seize with a win. You would have thought they would play the game as if it were the last in their careers, but instead of seizing the opportunity and beating the Oilers, the Jets were crushed, looking listless and inept.

They could not stop the Oilers' pass rush, which ran rampant over their offensive line. Their defense offered little resistance of the Houston offense.

They finished the season 8-8 and out of the playoffs. Again.

"It was an embarrassment," Jets cornerback James Hasty said after the game. "If anybody doesn't think it was an embarrassment, and they walk up to me and say that, I'll slap their face."

For Bruce Coslet, who had no idea he'd coached his last game as a Jet, it was a familiar place to end the season in disappointment. His only playoff season as the Jets' head coach ended in a 17-10 loss to the Oilers in the 1991 wild-card round.

"This is the first time this year that we got our rear handed to us," Coslet said after the 24-0 loss. "There was no turning point, no deciding point. They handled us handily."

Boomer Esiason, the Jets' quarterback, who went 0-7 in Houston while with the Cincinnati Bengals, said, "We didn't lose our playoff berth here at this stadium. We lost it a lot earlier in the season. There were so many games we could have won that this game shouldn't have mattered. But we probably saved our worst game for last."

And it was in Houston at the end of the season. Of course.

"CUT BRUCE LOOSE"

A column in *The New York Post* produced a huge headline, which ranted: "Fire Him!" on the back page and "Cut Bruce Loose" on the inside page where the story ran. The point of the column was simply that Bruce Coslet had taken the Jets as far as he could and that it was time for a change. Four years, no winning seasons and one wild-card playoff loss. It was time for Coslet to go.

Apparently, the Jets' management agreed with *The Post*'s assessment, and Coslet was fired shortly after the column ran.

Coslet was either a brilliant sun-splashed day or a deadly hurricane. There was never anything in between, and it affected the players, who—like him—lacked consistency.

After Coslet was fired, Boomer Esiason, the home-grown quarterback from Long Island whom Coslet had in Cincinnati and brought to New York, was livid, particularly at reporters whom he believed tried to bring Coslet down.

Pete Carroll, who was Coslet's defensive coordinator and close friend, was elevated to head coach. Little did he know how little time he would get before suffering the same fate as his friend and former boss.

"We never considered anyone else [other than Carroll], but we know him and he knows us," Steinberg said. "It's been a four-year interview."

Unfortunately, for Carroll, that four-year interview bought him only one year as the Jets' head coach.

2

PETE CARROLL

WITH PETE CARROLL came a different approach. There was a youthful enthusiasm that followed Carroll wherever he went, and there was a sense that because of the way he treated his players, they would do anything for him.

That, however, lasted only so long.

The installation of a basketball court alongside the practice field, the three-point shooting contests with players and coaches, the bowling outings, the penalty-kick soccer contest he conducted with U.S. soccer player Tony Meola, whom the team signed as an experiment, all turned out to mean nothing as he, like so many before him, failed to win.

Nothing would mark Carroll's downfall more than one game on a Sunday in November. It was a day from which neither Carroll, nor his players, nor the fans, nor the Jets' organization would recover for a long time.

"CLOCK! CLOCK! CLOCK!"

The Jets were 6-5 and ready to flex their muscles in the AFC East with the rival Miami Dolphins playing in their house—even though it was named Giants Stadium.

The Jets built leads of 17-0 and 24-6, and the house was rocking. A win and the Jets would be 7-5 and have a share of first place in the AFC East. After that, who knew how far they could go.

Then, before everyone's disbelieving eyes, everything went to hell.

Dan Marino, the Miami quarterback, was conducting a hurry-up offense attack on the Jets, who were leading 24-21. Once at the eight-yard line and with the clock down to less than 30 seconds remaining in the game, Marino was instructing his teammates to get set at the line of scrimmage so he could spike the ball to stop the clock.

"Clock! Clock! Clock!" he yelled as his players set.

With the Jets' defense expecting a spike and a breather, Marino took the snap and dropped two steps back. He didn't spike the ball. He tossed it to receiver Mark Ingram in the end zone for the game-winning touchdown with 22 seconds remaining. The Jets' defense stood in place and tried to figure out what had just happened.

Pete Carroll led the Jets for one season. His energetic approach was refreshing to his players, but there was not enough change on the gridiron to impact the final scores.

They were duped.

Dolphins 28, Jets 24.

AT A LOSS

Jets left tackle Jeff Criswell sat slumped on the stool in front of his locker, his voice barely audible. Criswell had felt disappointment before as a Jet, but this 28-24 loss to Miami was excruciating. The face on this 6-foot-7 behemoth was beet red. He looked like he was about to explode, but his ability to act on that angry energy was sapped from him by the shock of the loss.

"I'm at a loss for words right now," he said. "I'm frustrated. It's hard for me to believe."

"It's hard to put in words how you feel after a loss like this," Jets quarterback Boomer Esiason said. "You feel like your team has turned the corner, and you feel like it's coming around, and this kind of thing happens. You just hope we have enough character—and I'm sure we do—to bounce back."

They didn't, and they didn't.

Out with the loss went the character Esiason spoke about. The Jets would lose their final five games of the season.

Dolphins quarterback Dan Marino fades back to pass over the fooled Jets defense in Miami's 28-24 win in 1994. The Jets defenders thought Marino would spike the ball to stop the clock. Instead Marion fired the game-winning touchdown to Mark Ingram and the Jets were left scratching their heads.

HASTY RETREAT

The many years of losing have produced countless Jets players with gripes and unhappiness. None, however, suffered the kind of mental breakdown that cornerback James Hasty did in 1994. Seven years of losing with the Jets finally piled onto Hasty like a gang tackle, and finally he snapped.

"Who can deal with seven years of losing?" Hasty said with the Jets mired in a 6-9 record and about to close out the 1994 season at 6-10 with five consecutive losses. "I'm at a crossroads in my career. I've had a good season that's been overshadowed by what's happened on this club. I'm a free agent after this year, and what happens is in God's hands.

"I thought we'd be there this year. I thought we had the nucleus of people. We took care of getting an offensive coordinator, a wideout, and some more defensive linemen. I thought these would be taken care of. What player sits down and is pessimistic going into the season? I thought we had a legitimate chance of making the playoffs."

Things got ugly for Hasty late in the season as the end in New York neared for him. After safety Pat Terrell had blown his assignment and left Hasty in one-on-one coverage with San Diego Chargers receiver Tony Martin, who caught a 60-yard touchdown on the play, Hasty screamed at Terrell on the sideline. In the heat of the game, which was still in progress, Hasty stood inches

James Hasty sounded off about the losing seasons and behind-the-scenes struggles.

away from Terrell and berated him for his poor play, getting so close to physically harming Terrell that he had to be restrained by Jets players on the sideline, who separated the two.

Later, in the quiet of the loser's locker room, Hasty sought out Terrell and tried to smooth things over.

"I apologized to Pat for what occurred," Hasty said. "I don't know what people assumed. Maybe I'm supposed to deal with seven years of losing and just be the greatest guy in the world. I'm not able to be that kind of person. You see a person that's very frustrated when the games are lost. Who honestly can deal with seven years of losing? I don't know anybody who can deal with that who considers himself a competitor, who considers himself a winner.

"If my attitude is not right on the day we lose, I apologize. Seven years has taken its toll. If the Jets feel like it's time for James Hasty to move on or if James Hasty feels like it's time to move on, then so be it. I'm going to talk to my teammates and let them know how I feel about certain things. All I can do is hope they understand what seven years of frustration are all about."

Hasty, who joined the Jets in 1988, was a part of only one winning season—a false-hope 8-7-1 record in his rookie year. In the off-season, not long after his diatribe, Hasty was no longer a Jet, moving on to Kansas City, where he would resurrect his career and finish with a series of playoff seasons.

HOUSTON, WE HAVE A PROBLEM TAKE II

In 1994, Pete Carroll would unknowingly end his Jets head coaching career in Houston in yet another season finale to forget.

This time it was a Christmas Eve 24-10 loss to close out a 6-10 season.

What made this day even more morose was the pregame announcement to beat writers that general manager Dick Steinberg was suffering from stomach cancer. The announcement was made to reporters in the press box minutes before kickoff. Team president Steve Gutman and public relations director Frank Ramos gathered everyone around and delivered the grim news, which left a pall over everyone and certainly took any excitement over the game away.

"Everything that could have happened to this team has happened," said quarterback Boomer Esiason, who along with the rest of the team was informed of the news after the game by Carroll. "And then to find out about Dick, all the players looked at each other as if to say, 'What happened?'"

3

BOOMER ESIASON

ONLY IN NEW YORK

BOOMER ESIASON remembers the beginning of a tumultuous relationship with one unknown New York fan.

Before his first game against Denver, he was warming up in front of the Jets' bench when he heard this guy in the stands screaming his name.

"Hey, Boomer, it's great to have you here. It's great to have a hometown boy here. I'm Long Island, too," he said.

Defying his normal protocol of not reacting to people in the crowd, Esiason nodded and gave him a thumbs up.

That became a defining moment for both Esiason and the fan.

From then on at every home game for three years, the man sat in the same seat, shouting critiques and insults at Esiason.

During his last game against the Saints in 1995, there were about 20,000 fans in the stadium, but only one got Esiason's attention.

"Hey, Boomer, sorry it didn't work out. It's been great to have you here. You've handled yourself as a real class act and never made us feel bad that you were here," he yelled.

Then, Esiason recalled, the man started talking about Esiason's son, Gunnar, who has cystic fibrosis.

"I really hope your son is doing well," the guy said to Esiason.

Esiason was shocked at the man's concern. He decided to shake his hand and thank him.

As he reached out to grab the guy's hand, the man sneered, "You suck. Get the fuck out of town."

Needless to say, the guy never shook Esiason's hand.

It was a typical New York fan who couldn't wait to get the last word, according to Esiason.

Of course, the Jets lost the game, too.

TRAFFIC JAM

One of the biggest decisions a Jets player or coach is confronted with after a game at Giants Stadium (in New Jersey) is whether to take the George Washington Bridge or the Lincoln Tunnel through New York City to get back to Long Island, where the team trains and most of the players live. Traffic either way can be horrendous.

Boomer Esiason always had the most perspective in the Jets locker room.

So there was Boomer Esiason, who'd thrown a key interception to A.B. Brown, somewhat facilitating a Miami Dolphins comeback victory that afternoon in the devastating loss in the infamous Dan Marino "Fake Spike" game of November 1994, driving toward the Lincoln Tunnel and spinning through the radio dials seeking a traffic report when he came upon WFAN, the New York sports radio station.

"Boomer Esiason sucks," ranted one caller on WFAN.

"How could Boomer throw that interception?" screamed another.

"Boomer's got to go!" yelled yet another.

As he sat in the parking lot that the Lincoln Tunnel becomes after games, Esiason decided to torture himself by sticking with WFAN and listening to the angry Jets fans spew their venom.

"It was a complete disaster; people were calling in and ripping the shit out of me as if I was the only player who played the game for the Jets," recalled Esiason, who was thankful that his vehicle had tinted windows so that the drivers around him could not recognize him.

As Esiason sat in traffic and listened to his fans torch him, a car filled with drunken Jets fans, who were coming from the game, rammed into the car in front of them, which was in the lane adjacent to Esiason's car.

For a moment Esiason sat in his car and debated whether he should get out and help the female driver and lose his anonymity or sit tight and wait for the traffic to budge.

Esiason opted to get out of his car to try to help the woman, who was slumped over the steering wheel in her car. He banged on the window of her locked car to get her attention and see if she was okay.

After a few bangs, the woman came to and looked up.

"Boomer? Is that you?" she said.

"Yes, are you all right?" Esiason asked.

Without blinking an eye, she blurted out, "You guys suck. How did you lose that game?"

As Esiason spoke with the stunned woman, the drunken Jets fans from the car that did the rear-ending got out and asked him for autographs right in the middle of the highway.

"These four guys," Esiason said, "were probably [a few minutes earlier] on their cell phones—Tony or Vinny from Queens—calling into WFAN screaming, 'What was Boomer thinking when he threw that pass? He can't throw the ball!'"

4

RICH KOTITE

WHAT COULD GO WRONG did go wrong almost from the moment Rich Kotite was hired to be the head of the Jets' family by team owner Leon Hess.

His two-year reign as the Jets' head coach was packed with more calamity than most franchises endure in a lifetime. The end record for the Kotite Jets was 4-28.

DISCIPLINE DISCIPLES

One of Rich Kotite's immediate downfalls was hiring a weak staff of assistant coaches. Instead of bringing in a staff that would complement his hands-off, easy-going style, Kotite brought in a network of his buddies in the business, and it was like camp. Everyone seemed to be off in separate directions.

For example, Matty McIntyre, one of Kotite's assistants, used to house a keg of Budweiser in his dorm room during training camp. McIntyre would send John

Owner Leon Hess (right) named Rich Kotite (left) his coach to get the
Jets back on track in January 1995.

Nicholas, an operations assistant for the team, to the
liquor store to pick up a barrel, which would end up in
McIntyre's room in the coaches' dorm, where the
assistant coaches would pound beers in their off time.

McIntyre and the assistant coaches weren't the only
ones who imbibed, either. According to Nicholas,
Nicholas would go to the bodega on the Hempstead
Turnpike. He would grab 40-ouncers for the players
who requested them.

VANCE WHO?

Vance Joseph had gained some fame by throwing a
Hail Mary bomb to defeat Michigan while in college at
Colorado. Undrafted, he was signed as a free agent by
the Jets, who liked his athleticism. The Jets tried him at

cornerback, a position he'd never played before entering the NFL.

And Rich Kotite gave Joseph his first NFL start at cornerback against the Oakland Raiders and their Hall of Fame-bound receiver Tim Brown.

The result was—as you would have expected it to be—a Raiders rout, with Brown conducting a clinic in a 47-10 Oakland win over the bumbling Jets before a nighttime national television audience. Jeff Hostetler threw four touchdown passes, two of them against poor Joseph. Joseph looked like a high school player trying to cover one of the NFL's elite as he floundered around in the secondary, yards removed from Brown as the Raiders' receiver scampered for his two touchdowns.

As the Jets fell further into their abyss and the fourth quarter arrived, their fans chanted "Let's go, Raiders!"

Player reaction to the chants was disbelief as they looked up from the sidelines to the stands and watched the angry patrons chanting the other team's name.

Brown, who openly wondered why the Jets' coaches didn't at least give Joseph some help out there instead of leaving him in one-on-one man coverage, said, "It was strange out there. I started feeling bad for the Jets. I know it's not a good feeling."

IS IT PERSONAL OR PERSONNEL?

Among the trademarks of the Rich Kotite era were a number of personnel decisions that simply made you scratch your head.

One of the worst moves was his decision to give inexperienced Everett McIver his first NFL start at left tackle against the Buffalo Bills and their Hall of Fame-bound defensive end Bruce Smith, the league's all-time leader in quarterback sacks.

The result was the Jets' quarterback, Boomer Esiason, was on the ground lying unconscious for about two minutes before being carried off the field.

Esiason was knocked unconscious by a Smith hit, thanks to a McIver false-start penalty that was called by the referee but not heard by Smith, who whipped past the inept tackle and bludgeoned Esiason helmet to helmet. On the play, McIver looked frozen as Smith shot past him like an Amtrak train and collided with Esiason's helmet. It truly looked like Esiason was being hit by an oncoming car. It was that scary. You wondered if Esiason was ever going to get up. After the collision, McIver simply stood alone, seemingly dumbfounded at what had just transpired.

"I don't remember anything," Esiason said, who said the hit felt like a car accident.

"It was very scary," Smith said. "I have never taken part in a play that was so violent in my career. A thousand things were going through my mind. I just tried to deliver a blow and do my job, but at the same time, a part of me is saying, 'Why didn't I just push him down?' I'm just glad he's all right.

"I was surprised they left me one-on-one with him [McIver] so many times."

So were Esiason's teammates, who were rattled by the team's ineptitude and wondered aloud about some of the personnel decisions made by the coaching staff.

Further exasperating the Jets and their fans was Dexter Carter, who was a premier kick returner for the San Francisco 49ers but who had turned into a walking fumble machine once signed by the Jets. In the game in Buffalo, only the Jets' fifth game of the season, he lost a fumble for the third time of the year. This one came on a kickoff return just before halftime and was immediately converted to a Bills touchdown and a 16-3 halftime lead. The Jets were still in the game as Carter fielded the punt and tried to make a move up the field. He was hit. The ball popped loose. The Bills recovered. And suddenly a manageable six-point deficit became a 13-point hole and yet another rout was on at the expense of the hapless Jets.

Asked about Carter after the game, special teams coach Ken Rose said, "I'm too emotionally messed up to talk right now. I'm ready to explode."

END OF AN ERROR

On December 17, 1995, in their second to last game of the year, the Jets came to Houston again, but with their third head coach in three years. This time, a 23-6 loss to the Oilers gave the Jets a 3-12 record.

"I will be one happy camper when this place will not be housing a professional football team," quarterback Boomer Esiason said after the loss, referring to the Oilers' imminent move to Nashville. "As far as I'm

concerned, they can take this place and just play baseball in it."

The combined score of the three-season Houston debacle was Oilers 71, Jets 16. In this one, the Jets managed just 13 offensive yards in the first half. When at halftime in the Jets' locker room, players were saying, "Let's score," Jets left tackle Matt Willig got up off of the stool at his locker and attempted to boost some life and humor into his teammates by offering this more realistic advice: "Hey, let's get a first down."

After the game, Willig said, "We've lost a lot of ways, and we've played bad offensively for most of the year, but this has to be the worst. To have 13 yards in the first half is ridiculous."

These were Rich Kotite's words after the game: "This is about as bad as you're going to see."

Incredibly, though, it would get worse for the Jets. A lot worse.

"STUNNED AND AMAZED"

Once the Jets spent gads of money on a new quarterback, Neil O'Donnell, who was coming off playing in Super Bowl XXX, and two expensive tackles, Jumbo Elliott and David Williams, they thought all would be better in 1996 after Rich Kotite's disastrous 3-13 season in 1995.

It wasn't.

It started in Denver with yet another questionable personnel decision. With both expensive tackles out

Quarterback Neil O'Donnell had a rough time leading the Jets.

with tweaked hamstring injuries, which occurred even before training camp began, career guard Roger Duffy was asked to start at right tackle. Duffy wasn't told of the position switch officially until right before the game, because the coaches still held out hope that one of the tackles might be able to play.

After the Jets' 31-6 loss to the Broncos in a game during which the Jets' offensive line showed little resistance and O'Donnell was harassed by the Denver pass rush all day, Duffy was asked what his reaction was to the start at tackle. "Stunned and amazed," he said. Duffy, who was usually such a low-key guy he appeared catatonic, was actually animated, raising his eyebrows at the thought of playing tackle in an NFL game for the first time.

"HERE WE GO AGAIN"

Neil O'Donnell, who was signed for $25 million, probably would have given every cent of it back not to go through the pain and anguish he endured.

By the time December 1, 1996, came, O'Donnell had already missed seven games with a dislocated throwing shoulder in what was a record-setting losing season. Four games remained, and he was medically healthy enough to return, so he did. He was to start against the Houston Oilers at Giants Stadium with the team already mired in a 1-11 record.

As it turned out, O'Donnell should never have left the house on December 1, 1996. Warming up well before the game, O'Donnell popped the calf muscle in his right leg while having a soft toss with backup quarterback Frank Reich.

Honest.

"What else can go wrong?" O'Donnell asked Pat Kirwan, the team's director of player administration, as he was helped into the locker room.

"I saw his facial expression and saw his body language, and I knew something was wrong," Reich recalled. "I turned to [third-string quarterback Glenn] Foley and said, 'Here we go again.'"

"It was the first adversity we'd ever met before the game started," Rich Kotite said. "In my wildest dreams I wouldn't have thought it would happen. He was all by himself when it happened. Someone tapped me on the shoulder before pregame warmups. The offensive linemen were coming into the end zone, and I saw Neil being carried off in the other end zone, and I got on a walkie-talkie and was told his calf muscle was pulled."

The bumbling Jets ended up losing the game, 35-10 before 21,723 fans, a record 55,985 no-shows at Giants Stadium. The embarrassing beat goes on.

As he lumbered off the field after the loss, Kotite was hit with a full cup of beer.

"I've been doused before," he said. "I had a GORE-TEX jacket on. I couldn't tell."

NOT QUITTING, NOT FIRED, STEPPING DOWN

Rich Kotite, from the moment he was named as the "head of the Jets' family" by Leon Hess, created a conflict in reporters.

The fact that he was such a nice man made it difficult to rip him for the inferior job he was doing. Yet his clear deficiencies as a head coach made it difficult not to break him down, because the team's degree of inferiority was so staggering it was impossible to ignore.

The Jets lost 28 of the 32 games Kotite coached in his two seasons. They were both blowouts and close games, but like the "Bad News Bears," they were always entertaining. It was always something with the Kotite Jets.

And Kotite's departure from the team was, fittingly, entertaining to the very end.

At the press conference inside Weeb Ewbank Hall, Kotite refused to acknowledge that he was being fired or that he was quitting.

Kotite lumbered up to the podium in the quiet auditorium and kept his composure so well, you'd have thought he was making a routine announcement. He didn't seem nervous. He wasn't showing any signs of emotion. He was almost cold.

"I wasn't fired; I didn't quit," Kotite said defiantly. "I'm stepping down."

In typical unorthodox Kotitian manner, Kotite "stepped down" days before the Jets' final game of the

1996 season but wanted to coach that final game, a home matchup against the Miami Dolphins.

Saddled with a 1-14 record at the time and having lost six in a row, the Jets lost 31-28 that day, losing a lead in the process, the sixth squandered halftime lead of the season.

As Kotite walked through the Giants Stadium tunnel for the last time, he wasn't showered with cheap, flat beer, the way he'd been several weeks earlier, but one fan did hang a sign prominently, which read: "THE END OF AN ERROR."

Kotite departed with a 4-28 record, tied with the Tampa Bay Buccaneers' Leeman Bennett for the worst winning percentage (.125) for any coach with at least 30 games with one team. Kotite finished with 19 losses in his last 20 games. His failure as a head coach even dated back to a seven-game losing streak with the Eagles before he was fired in Philadelphia, meaning he won only four games in his last 39 games as a head coach.

"I think the greatest lessons in life are learned in tough times and I think this football team, to a man, is going to take something positive away from this year," Kotite said after his final game as a football coach. "I think it's going to come to serve them individually and collectively. I believe that."

Sadly, the first best thing that would serve this wounded franchise would be Kotite's departure.

"It's been a poor two years," Kotite said.

NO SORROW

Rich Kotite never wanted anyone to feel sorry for him. He always pointed out that he was given the chance to live a dream even if he never got to ride it over the rainbow.

"I've been very fortunate," Kotite said of his failed tenure as the head coach of the team he used to play for. "I'm the only guy who came out of my college [Wagner College in Staten Island] who ever played in the NFL. I had two opportunities as a head coach. I'm a very lucky guy; I really am."

Days earlier, at his infamous "stepping down" press conference, Kotite said, "I feel I've always been a bottom-line guy, and when you're 3-13 and 1-14, that just doesn't cut it. I really don't want to lose the fans for this organization. You have to do something to show them."

It was difficult to believe things could get worse than they were under Joe Walton, Bruce Coslet, and Pete Carroll, but they actually did under Kotite.

Shortly after Kotite's departure, though, Leon Hess would make one final move before his death, sending the Jets toward what seemed to be football civilization.

Enter Bill Parcells.

5

LEON HESS

THE JETS' DIGNIFIED AND CLASSY OWNER,
who died in 2000, was always like Greta Garbo in that he
was rather reclusive, particularly when it came to his
football team. Leon Hess let his football people make
the day-to-day decisions and trusted their judgment.

A TROPICAL EPIPHANY

Leon Hess had been vacationing in the Bahamas
when he was told by his daughter that Rich Kotite had
been fired. Hess said he got an "eerie feeling," adding,
"I went inside, turned on the TV, and I saw a picture of
Rich Kotite being fired." He promptly called his team
president, Steve Gutman, and asked for Kotite's
telephone number.

To Kotite—who probably figured he'd never get
another head coaching job again, though he was
reportedly a candidate for the Carolina Panthers job—

it must have been as though he won the lottery with a found ticket.

"I called Rich and said, 'Please don't do anything. Wait until I come home, or I'll come home tomorrow if you want to do something,'" Hess recalled of his conversation with Kotite. "He said he'd wait."

Kotite even admitted shock, saying he thought Hess' call was a prank.

"I thought it was someone pretending to be him," Kotite said. "But when the operator said it was the overseas Hess operator, I knew it was the real thing."

Kotite, a Brooklyn native and Staten Island resident, called his homecoming a "dream come true."

"For some reason, I feel it in my bones," he said. "The timing is right for this."

"I'M 80 YEARS OLD, AND I WANT RESULTS NOW"

Without question, Leon Hess' most colorful public moment came when he made his appearance at the press conference announcing the hiring of Rich Kotite in January 1995.

Not only was Hess present at the press conference, he was the star of the show, working the auditorium upstairs at Weeb Ewbank Hall like George Burns used to work the best rooms in comedy.

"I'm 80 years old, and I want results now," Hess barked to his stunned audience in his first news

Owner Leon Hess wanted his Jets to win.

conference since 1988 and only the second in his life. "I've waited for 25 years. The buck stops with me. I'm just one of those fans who has been disappointed for 25 years. Let's make a change. If it's wrong, it's my fault. But at least I'm doing something for the fans and trying to do something for myself at 80. I'm entitled to some enjoyment from this team, and that means winning."

Hess anointed Kotite having no possible idea at the moment what a colossal mistake he was making.

The headline writers at *The New York Post*, however, smelled out the rat. Blaring to readers in all editions read the front-page headline in big, black block letters: "Dumb and Dumber," referring to the ouster of Pete Carroll and the hiring of Kotite.

Hess, too, made a thinly veiled jab at Carroll, whose team clearly had players that dogged it late in the season, saying, "The Jets family doesn't quit."

"HORSES' ASSES"

Every year, Leon Hess visits his team's Thanksgiving Day practice.

Hess rarely attended team practices and wasn't even at every game during the regular season, but he never missed Thanksgiving, usually arriving in a black Town Car and often with family members. It was the only time of the year when the reclusive owner made himself available to talk. His words, though always brief, were always cordial.

Regardless of the weather or the whereabouts of his team in the AFC East standings, Hess would always gather the players together after their Thanksgiving Day practice and say a few words.

No Thanksgiving was more memorable than the one in 1995 when, on a cloudy, chilly day with his team stalled at 2-9 and readying themselves for a weekend trip to Seattle to play the Seahawks, Hess tried to rally his troops with these incredible words: "Let's go out with dignity and show 'em we're not horses' asses."

Mixed in with the amusement of the 81-year-old man's stunning words were cheers from the players. Here was the Jets' reclusive owner surrounded by a bunch of 300-pound football players who were completely captivated by his words and went on to beat the Seahawks 16-10.

It turned out to be an eventful rest of the season—with the team's affairs unfolding in ways that reminded fans of the words from Hess' Thanksgiving speech.

Within hours of Hess' famous Thanksgiving Day rallying cry, Carlton Haselrig, the Jets' troubled right guard, failed an NFL drug test and checked into a rehabilitation facility. He would later leave the rehab facility and disappear for weeks, prompting his wife, Sara, to plead with him to return in an article in *The New York Post.*

The Jets had three players—defensive end Marvin Washington, defensive tackle Erik Howard, and linebacker Marvin Jones—fined a total of $31,500 for what the NFL determined as dangerous hits on opposing quarterbacks.

Jets kicker Nick Lowery, perhaps one of the most erudite and charitable players in the game, was accused of slapping a 20-year-old New England Patriots ballboy after the two cursed each other out when Lowery told the ballboy he was handing out cold footballs for him to kick.

They also lost their final four games of the season to finish what was then the worst record in franchise history at 3-13.

AGGRESSIVE NEGOTIATIONS

One of the most memorable moments Leon Hess delivered came the day he hired Bill Parcells to coach the team. It would be not only the best and most important move he ever made with the team, but it would also be the final major decision he would make with his team before dying.

On the day he announced Parcells as his new coach, Hess made a rare appearance before the media. He truly appeared to be enjoying the moment, regaling the press with stories of his youth on the New Jersey Shore, where Parcells spent much of his life.

Hess, who made his fortune in the oil business, said the hiring of Parcells was a little more fun than sitting across the table discussing oil deals in the Middle East with Colonel Muammar al-Qadhafi.

"Many years ago I had a meeting in Libya, and a revolver was put on the table," Hess recalled with a smirk. He paused for a dramatic moment and then added, "I'm here."

This was Hess' way of showing the kind of survivor he was. It, too, was his way of saying that he was not going to back down from the Patriots and their efforts to thwart the Jets from getting Parcells, who was Hess' man all along.

6

BILL PARCELLS

THERE WAS ONLY ONE MAN FOR THE JETS to turn to once the harsh realization that Rich Kotite wasn't the man to lead them to the promised land set in, and that man was none other than Bill Parcells.

Parcells' relationship with Patriots owner Robert Kraft was crumbling, and the tempestuous coach wanted out. With prodding from all corners team owner Leon Hess, 82 at the time, made his move and landed the Big Tuna. His troubled franchise would finally find some pride and glory, albeit fleeting, before his death.

Unlike any other coach in recent history, Parcells arrived at the Jets' doorstep with credentials. He won two Super Bowls with the Giants and was coming off a Super Bowl loss with New England. So when Parcells came, he came with a wrecking ball and an attitude. He tore apart the roster, shut out the media from everywhere with eight-foot-high fences that barred

anyone from roaming into the player parking lots and the practice fields.

"This is my last job," Parcells declared with a sincere look on his face. "After this, I'll ride off into the sunset."

As compensation for wresting Parcells from New England, decided by NFL commissioner Paul Tagliabue, who acted as an arbitrator, the Patriots received the Jets' third- and fourth-round picks in the 1997 draft, plus the Jets' second-round draft pick in 1998 and first-round pick in 1999.

It was the greatest deal the Jets made in their history. Parcells brought them from the dark ages to respectability. And although some bad things have happened since his hiring and departure, the organization has always been competitive and didn't suffer a losing season until it went 6-10 in 2003.

GROCERY SHOPPING

Getting Bill Parcells was hardly easy for the Jets.

Before Parcells was actually able to become the Jets' head coach, he was initially forced by Tagliabue to be a "consultant" for a year before he could coach again.

The Patriots, at the time, weren't even happy about that, with New England owner Robert Kraft calling the arrangement "a transparent farce."

"It's like rules don't matter for the Jets and Bill Parcells," Kraft said.

Bill Parcells changed the entire mood of the team, from one of disappointment to one of determination. His leadership began to turn the Jets organization around.

Kraft claimed the Jets negotiated with Parcells while the Patriots were still playing in the 1996 season, a practice called tampering and highly illegal in the NFL, though difficult to prove.

Kraft also believed that Parcells would never last in the consulting position, predicting that he couldn't stay out of the media spotlight for an entire year.

"Those press conferences he conducts every day," Kraft said, "those are like a narcotic to Bill Parcells. He won't be able to stay away. Those are like a drug to him."

In the meantime, while Parcells was to "consult," Bill Belichick, his top lieutenant, was named the head coach, and it turned out to be the briefest head-coaching reign in NFL history—six days.

Belichick never coached a game, joking once Parcells was ruled to be able to be named head coach, "I'm stepping down with an undefeated record, untied, unscored upon, no kickoff returns allowed for touchdowns, and no PATs blocked."

In essence, Belichick's stint as head coach was as a pawn in a high-stakes chess game of chicken between the Jets and the Patriots.

Parcells' biggest beef with Kraft in New England was what he perceived as the owner's meddling in football personnel matters.

"If you're going to cook the meal," Parcells often when referring to the power structure of coaching and having final say on personnel decisions, "you should be able to buy the groceries."

CULTURE SHOCK

Carl Banks, a former Pro Bowl linebacker with the Giants under Bill Parcells, recalled the first day he arrived at the Jets' facility as a part of Parcells' staff.

Banks sat in Parcells' office and thought about what he was seeing inside Weeb Ewbank Hall. As he walked through the building, he noticed that the atmosphere was morose and laid back. Secretaries, nonessential football personnel, and football staffers were wandering around the building unfocused and unmotivated. It was as though they were more concerned with their own agendas than with football or the Jets organization. Banks had never seen anything like it.

"This whole culture has to change," Parcells said, confirming exactly what Banks thought. "Banksy, there's a lot of work here, but the cupboard's not bare."

Parcells' first move was to lock everyone out, beginning with the media, building fences around the complex and putting in security codes for people to use to get into the building.

The next move he made was to define football operations and non-football operations, thus defining his coaching staff and all essential personnel and all those who weren't related to the definitive football decisions and then separating them within the building. Those who had nothing to do with what took place on the field were pushed to another part of the building right away.

"They were no longer roaming the halls and glad-handing," Banks said.

Discipline had arrived along with the strong arm of the Parcells regime, and there was no longer a laid-back feel to the building, with office workers hanging out chatting away when there was work to be done. It was all business.

FIRST IMPRESSIONS

The first compelling player-coach showdown was going to be Bill Parcells and Keyshawn Johnson, the brash young millionaire receiver who was fresh off writing a book that ripped coaches and teammates.

"The immediate concern was how was he going to deal with Keyshawn Johnson," Carl Banks recalled. "He'd just written a book. To his credit, Bill took a minute to find out who Keyshawn Johnson was. It's just like having a substitute teacher. Students behave differently for the substitute than they do for the real teacher, and the real teacher was in the house in the way of Parcells."

On Parcells' second day with the Jets, he first made contact with Johnson in the weight room. Parcells marched right over to Johnson and said hello to him. Then he proceeded to start ribbing him, telling him he looked a little overweight and offering several other uncomplimentary jabs along with it, such as questioning his workout habits and whether he had the toughness to be a receiver for him. Clearly, Parcells was testing Johnson in this early meeting.

Bill Parcells made sure early on that Keyshawn Johnson knew who was in charge.

Banks, who witnessed the pow-wow, called it "one of those break-the-ice moments."

"It wasn't, 'Hey jerk, I'm Bill Parcells and you better get on board,'" Banks said. "They hit it off right away. From the look of Keyshawn when Bill started walking toward him, it didn't look like they'd had much of a conversation before that. Keyshawn was notorious for not wanting to work out. Bill broke the ice with him, and the relationship started to build from there."

THE WRATH OF BILL

One day during the early part of Bill Parcells' reign with the Jets, Mike Kensil, the team's director of operations, happened to be walking to practice with Parcells and Carl Banks when the head coach suddenly went off on Kensil, ranting about things weren't being done the way he wanted them done.

"It was one of Bill's moments," said Banks, who had been with Parcells since Banks was a player and had incurred the wrath of the control-freak coach and his bipolar-like personality. "Mike just happened to be the guy that was standing there, and he was ripped about anything and everything . . . Mike is like a Boy Scout. He's trying to do nothing wrong. He's just trying to please the head coach, and all of a sudden Parcells is giving him a laundry list of what the hell was wrong and starts ripping him up and down."

Almost in tears, Kensil was shocked. He was visibly shaken, looking like a child who'd just been scolded by his father. He stood there wondering what he had done to incur Parcells' wrath. As soon as Parcells walked away, Banks gave Kensil a firm pat on the back.

"Mike, don't worry about it. It was just your day today," he said as he left Kensil in the hallway.

NOT JUST FOR THE EXECUTIVES

Carl Banks, too, recalled the way Bill Parcells would tear apart his own assistant coaches in front of the players in practice.

"He's been notorious in practice for calling all of his coaches into an impromptu meeting and ripping them all new assholes right in the middle of practice," Banks said. "I've seen a few coaches get fired on the spot. Belichick has been fired a number of times in practice."

DON'T BELONG HERE

Bill Parcells was also notorious for his closed practices. No one from the entire building, even management, was allowed to watch practice. Carl Banks recalled some times when a marketing guy or the team president Steve Gutman would bring one of his muckety-mucks into the practice bubble to show them around. Parcells would be seething.

"You know what people call that 1,000-yard stare?" Banks said. "Bill had an infamous 52-yard stare, we called it. When the guys from operations came into the practice bubble, like [public relations director] Frank Ramos, [director of business operations] Bob Parente, guys from the other side of the office, and practice was going on, all of a sudden Bill would stop practice and start staring, and guys started heading toward the door. His stare was kind of like a 'You don't fucking belong here' look."

Parcells' look was utterly demeaning, like a parent looking upon his child with complete disdain before sending the kid to his room.

"I remember Steve Gutman used to bring his guys in and parade them around," Banks said. "Once they started to move a little closer to the action, Bill would stop what he was doing and just stare from one sideline to the opposite sideline, 52 yards. He just looked and kept looking until their asses started to move toward the door. It was the most intense thing."

MOWED DOWN BY MOTOWN

The Detroit Lions have left an indelible red mark on the Jets on more than one occasion.

But with Bill Parcells at the helm in his first season in 1997, the Jets went to Detroit to play the Lions in a game that, if the team won, would send the Jets to the playoffs just one season after finishing 1-15 under Rich Kotite. It was the season finale for both teams, and it was a game in which Barry Sanders would eclipse the 2,000-yard rushing mark for a season.

The Jets gave the game away.

"I always tell [the players], 'Don't you be the guy that sends your team home. How would you feel if you were the guy that did it?'" Parcells said.

Well, in this game, ultimately a 13-10 loss, three players cost the Jets a chance at a historic playoff berth after one of the worst seasons in NFL history. Running back Leon Johnson, on a halfback option pass to the end zone, threw a critical interception.

"It was poor judgment by Leon on that throw," Parcells said of the halfback option pass, indicating that he should have thrown the ball into the third row of the stands. "We've been practicing that play since the first day."

Fullback Richie Anderson, who for all the good he did in his career with the Jets always seemed to make his worst mistakes in the throes of the most pressure-filled situations, let a Neil O'Donnell pass bounce off his hands for another crucial Lions interception.

Finally, little-used reserve quarterback Ray Lucas, a Parcells favorite, was thrust into the game for O'Donnell, not a Parcells favorite.

Most questionable was Parcells' use of Lucas, who had been nothing more than a mad-dog special teams player. To use him in such a critical situation with the season on the line raised serious questions about Parcells' confidence in O'Donnell, who privately fumed at the benching. Earlier in the season Parcells had shown signs of not being enamored of O'Donnell as his quarterback, and there was little love lost between the two. A Lucas interception cost the Jets dearly in a low-scoring game. But do you blame the inexperienced Lucas or Parcells for putting him in that position?

In a sense, Parcells was one of those people he preached about "sending" his team "home."

"I messed up," Lucas said. "I didn't make the right decision. When you come this far, one play doesn't win or lose the game, but I can't stomach the fact that I let Coach Parcells down. It makes me sick to my stomach."

When Parcells was asked whether he had slighted O'Donnell by using Lucas, he said, "Only an idiot would see it that way, only a fool. You use what you have."

The loss dropped the Jets to 9-7 and eliminated them from the playoffs.

FINALLY, GLORY

After what happened in the magical 1998 season, every Jets fan on the planet was ready to name Bill Parcells king of the world. There was the 12-4 regular-season record. There was the first-ever division title in franchise history. There was even playoff glory, the best of which came at home, where the Jets have never really enjoyed a lot of glory.

The Jets' 34-24 win over the Jacksonville Jaguars at Giants Stadium represented the greatest moment in the franchise's tortured history since Joe Namath in Super Bowl III. Giants Stadium rocked for the Jets game like it had never rocked for a Jets game. The atmosphere was positively electric, the sounds louder than the Jets had ever experienced for a home game.

The Jets' win in that game sent them to the AFC championship game in Denver, where they would find themselves 60 minutes from reaching the Super Bowl for only the second time in franchise history.

The Jets figured they weren't done despite the fact that they were still only two years removed from 1-15.

"Now," Jets veteran equipment manager Bill Hampton Sr., one of only three people at the time still with the organization who was a part of the 1969 miracle, "anything can happen."

Then, referring to Parcells and his defensive genius lieutenant Bill Belichick, Hampton added, "With those two guys, anything can happen."

Wayne Chrebet, who grew up about five miles from Giants Stadium, said, "I used to come here when the Giants were in the playoffs. I think this was a little louder, because these Jets fans have waited so long."

MILE-HIGH MISERY

The Jets' meteoric rise under Bill Parcells was so dramatic it was difficult to truly measure during its defining moments.

Just two years after he took over Rich Kotite's 1-15 mess, the Jets not only found themselves in the AFC championship game against the Broncos in Denver, but they were leading at halftime. With 11:56 remaining in the third quarter of that game, the Jets led 10-0, meaning they were actually 26:56 away from a Super Bowl berth.

Then the ball dropped—six times.

Curtis Martin, who fumbles away the football as often as politicians tell the actual truth, fumbled away a crucial second-half possession. So did veteran fullback Keith Byars. Veteran returner Dave Meggett, who had been an integral part of the Giants' second Super Bowl win under Parcells, also made a costly gaffe in the form of a muffed kickoff.

In 11 minutes and 30 seconds, though, the game went from a 10-0 Jets lead to a 20-10 Broncos lead. And what began as redemption turned into just a tease for New York's most tortured franchise.

THE AFTERMATH OF DEFEAT

After the 20-10 loss to the Broncos, there were tears in the Jets' locker room, but there was a sense of going places, too, a feeling that hadn't truly gripped this organization in years.

"This wasn't baby steps," Bill Parcells said after the game. "This was a quantum leap for this team, about as far as you can jump. I think it compares favorably with any team in history over a two-year period. I'm not saying that from an egotistical standpoint, but from an accomplishment standpoint on the players' part. I can't put aside what these players have accomplished."

That hardly eased the players' pain.

"All I can think about right now is how close we were," Jets cornerback Ray Mickens said. "We were so close. One more game to win and you go to 'The Show,' and now we have to start all over again. It's so tough to think about."

Vinny Testaverde said, "I won't be satisfied until I win a championship. Everyone will say it's nice to close like we did, but this still hurts."

The Jets players, who only hours before had a swagger to them as they thought Super Bowl, looked drained and empty when they spoke. There was a feeling of unfinished business, unfulfilled dreams, and it showed in the faces of the players in that morgue-like visitor's locker room as they attempted to put words together to describe their feelings.

"This is why you train so hard in the off-season and work so hard in camp," Curtis Martin said. "This is what all the sprints and all the hitting and all the pain is for. We got here and didn't get the job done. It's all for naught if you don't make the Super Bowl. Hopefully, we can get back to this game and get to the Super Bowl."

They haven't come close since.

SO CLOSE, YET . . .

Carl Banks, the former Giants linebacker who worked under Bill Parcells on his Jets staff, recalled how broken up Parcells was after the championship game loss to the Broncos.

In the end, there were gaffes by the players Parcells counted on most. Running backs Curtis Martin, Keith Byars, and Dave Meggett were all responsible for game-turning turnovers, the things in the game that always made Parcells gray faster.

Banks remembered the sick look on Parcells' face as he boarded the team bus that night after the loss.

Parcells sat in the front right seat of the first team bus, and he looked much older than his years. His skin seemed paler than usual. There were bags under his eyes. His usually expression-rich face was blank, showing no emotion but emptiness.

"Games like that are the ones that tear guys like Bill Parcells apart, because you fight so hard to get there and you see things start to turn for the worse, some bad plays that you'd really practiced against, and it all goes wrong," Banks said."That was absolutely one of the toughest losses on him. He'd rather get blown out and not be good enough than have the tools and be so close and have a lot of breakdowns from guys that he normally could depend on."

VINNY'S ACHILLES HEEL

All of the positive feelings that the Jets carried with them in the off-season following the heartbreaking AFC championship game loss in Denver were torn apart quickly in the Jets' 1999 season opener. An off-season of beliefs that 1999 was going to be the Jets' year to return to the Super Bowl were dashed in the opening minutes of their 1999 season opener against the New England Patriots at Giants Stadium.

The sight of quarterback Vinny Testaverde crumpled on the Giants Stadium carpet blindly feeling for the back of his leg the way a fallen boxer feels

Quarterback Vinny Testaverde is helped off the field by Jets training personnel. The normally durable quarterback's injury resulted in the end of promise for the 1999 season.

around for his mouthpiece after being knocked to the canvas was jarring. It's a sight Jets fans will never forget.

Testaverde, who performed like an MVP in 1998, throwing 29 touchdown passes and only seven interceptions, ruptured his left Achilles tendon, shelving him for the season and leaving no capable backup to lead the charge.

The end result that September afternoon was a 30-28 loss to the Patriots, but the Jets lost much more. They lost all of the hope that has been stored up since the near miss in Denver the previous January.

"Vinny is so durable he's the type of player who usually gets right back up," Jets running back Curtis Martin said. "When I saw him lying there for such a long time, I knew it was something serious. Things happen sometimes. We don't know why. But you'll hurt your brain trying to figure it out."

Following the loss to the Patriots, Jets receiver Keyshawn Johnson cried while walking through the stadium tunnel.

"Not in a million years did I ever think I'd lose my starting quarterback for the season," Johnson said. "Right now, I don't even know what the hell to say. Shit. What can you do? You can't do shit. Nothing."

Johnson then pounded his fist on the podium and walked out of the room.

THE END?

Following the crushing loss to the Patriots, Bill Parcells was as resilient as he hoped his team would be in the face of such horrible fate. He, after all, had an entire season to coach and there were 52 other players in his locker room who needed to be assured that all hope was not lost.

Parcells was grim-faced in the postgame press conference. Deep down inside, he knew his season was sabotaged, but he could not show weakness or any sign of feeling sorry for himself.

That's why, when asked if he thought the season was "ruined," Parcells's back stiffened and he scoffed at the notion.

"I wouldn't say that," he snapped. "Why would I say that? What do you think, I'm going to put the white flag up? I'm not doing that."

He might as well have. He had left himself with only Rick Mirer and a very inexperienced Ray Lucas as reserve quarterbacks.

It was one of Parcells' most gross personnel miscalculations, perhaps born of the fact that Testaverde had been so durable throughout his career.

The Jets would stagger to a 2-6 start and rally to 8-8, but none of it really mattered. The season was lost on that September day.

BAY AREA BLUES

The maddening string began on October 24, 1999, to be exact. Six Jets games in Oakland in just four years. Most of those meetings would produce nightmarish moments.

The first of the string came under Bill Parcells' watch, but they surged to a 20-3 lead and looked like they would blow out the Raiders in their own backyard. Slowly and agonizingly, though, the Jets' lead disintegrated with defensive breakdowns one after another, particularly in the secondary, where cornerback Marcus Coleman was torched for a pivotal long pass instead of merely keeping the receiver in front of him to prevent a big play and protect the big lead.

Soon, that 20-3 lead became a 23-17 lead with the Jets clinging to hope and the Raiders in possession of the ball in the final seconds.

The final touchdown came with 26 seconds remaining when Raiders quarterback Rich Gannon scrambled around for what seemed to be minutes, eluding Jets linebacker Mo Lewis and drilling a five-yard touchdown pass to James Jett for the win.

"Yeah, I got my arms around him," Lewis said. "But it wasn't enough. It wasn't enough."

It never seemed to be enough for the Jets, who after allowing Raiders scoring drives of 72, 83, and 90 yards in the final 15 minutes of the game blew their a fourth-quarter lead for the fourth time in seven games and dropped to 1-6.

GOODBYE, BILL

All good things must come to an end. But why this soon? Why before the job was completed?

These were things Jets fans were left to wonder after Bill Parcells "retired" from coaching the team after only three seasons following the 1999 season that was wrecked by quarterback Vinny Testaverde's torn Achilles tendon in the first game of the season.

It's difficult to chastise Parcells for the job he did with the Jets in his three years, because he took them from Rich Kotite's 4-28 record in 1995 and 1996 and brought them as close to the glory of the Joe Namath Super Bowl as they've been since that historic moment in franchise history.

As much as Parcells restored pride and hope within the previously beleaguered organization, he, too, abandoned it at a time when its fans begged him to stay on and finish what he started.

Standing before his entire team inside the auditorium at Weeb Ewbank Hall, Parcells told his players the day after the 1999 season ended that he would be retiring, leaving them so stunned their jaws were dropped to the floor. The room was dead silent, never so quiet with 60 men in one room. It was in that auditorium that Parcells read a 1934 poem by Peter "Dale" Wimbrow Sr. called "The Guy in the Glass," which deals with the idea of never lying to the guy you see every morning in the mirror. As he read, players sat in stunned silence, some looking at each other quizzically.

The following is the text to Parcells' slightly altered version of the original poem, which he called, "The Man in the Glass."

WHEN YOU GET WHAT YOU WANT IN YOUR STRUGGLE FOR SELF
AND THE WORLD MAKES YOU KING FOR A DAY
JUST GO TO A MIRROR AND LOOK AT YOURSELF
AND SEE WHAT THAT MAN HAS TO SAY

FOR IT ISN'T YOUR FATHER, MOTHER OR WIFE
WHOSE JUDGMENT UPON YOU MUST PASS
THE FELLOW WHOSE VERDICT COUNTS MOST IN YOUR LIFE
IS THE ONE STARING BACK FROM THE GLASS

SOME PEOPLE MAY THINK YOU ARE A STRAIGHT-SHOOTIN' CHUM
AND CALL YOU A WONDERFUL GUY
BUT THE MAN IN THE GLASS SAYS YOU'RE ONLY A BUM
IF YOU CAN'T LOOK HIM STRAIGHT IN THE EYE

HE'S THE FELLOW TO PLEASE, NEVER MIND ALL THE REST
FOR HE'S WITH YOU CLEAR UP TO THE END
AND YOU'VE PASSED YOUR MOST DANGEROUS, DIFFICULT TEST
IF THE MAN IN THE GLASS IS YOUR FRIEND

YOU MAY FOOL THE WHOLE WORLD DOWN THE PATHWAY OF LIFE
AND GET PATS ON THE BACK AS YOU PASS
BUT YOUR FINAL REWARD WILL BE HEARTACHES AND TEARS
IF YOU'VE CHEATED THE MAN IN THE GLASS.

After the recitation, Parcells dropped the microphone and walked out of the silent locker room, leaving his players speechless and in a state of shock.

The poem and the gravity of Parcells' shocking announcement left his players slack-jawed as they looked around the quiet room at each other as if to say, "What now? Who's going to lead us now?"

"There were a lot of emotions throughout the room," safety Victor Green said. "No one wanted to see this happen right now."

CHALK IT UP

Later, Bill Parcells told reporters, he wasn't going to coach anywhere else, adding with his usual smugness, "You can write that on your chalkboard."

Parcells told reporters that he quit because he no longer felt up to the demands of a "365-day-a-year job."

He stood in the press room before a packed house and looked comfortable with himself and the decision he was announcing.

"Could I coach 16 more games?" he asked rhetorically. "Yeah, I could probably do it, or 32, or 48. But you have to have the committed effort to do it. I demanded a lot from the players, and they have a right to expect the same from me. And at this point in time, I just don't feel like I could give [what] I know has to be given to be successful.

"There won't be any coaching rumors about Bill Parcells, because I've coached my last game."

MISS YOU

In the years following Bill Parcells' departure, a testimony to how strong his personality is comes through when his former players continue to talk about him.

The debate about whether Parcells failed to finish the job with the Jets or whether he did what he could do before departing still rages on.

"We wanted him to come back, but everyone's got their own life they want to live a different way," Jets nose tackle Jason Ferguson said. "I feel no betrayal. I'm very appreciative of what he's done for me. He brought me into this league, and I learned a lot from him."

Jets cornerback Ray Mickens said he understands the feelings of the Jets fans who believe Parcells left too early, saying, "It kind of hurt to see him go. I really enjoyed he and [Bill] Belichick coaching here and playing under those guys. But change is imminent in this game. It's going to happen."

Both Mickens and Ferguson, though, said they knew the day Parcells left the Jets he wasn't finished coaching.

"He tried to stay out of [successor] Al Groh's way, but he came around to talk to certain players," Ferguson said of the year Parcells was in the front office after he stopped coaching. "He'd get on you for bad habits, call you 'she.' You still felt like he was the head coach, really. It was like he never left when he was up in the office. You knew he was coming back. He just had to get his people together. I knew he wanted to coach again. He still had that desire."

Mickens recalled those moments while Parcells was in the front office when he'd show signs of wanting to coach again.

"He had the itch," Mickens said. "I remember him pulling me over to the side and coaching me up. Things like that and being visible were indications that he missed the game. For him to leave here and say he was never going to coach again, you really couldn't put all your apples in that basket. He really loves football, and he missed it."

NEW YORK PERSPECTIVE

Carl Banks has cashed checks from both Jets and Giants.

He's also a very intelligent, well-thought-out man with incredibly keen perspective. He's lived his life in Giants skin as a player and Jets skin as a part of Bill Parcells' football staff and has felt the very divergent vibe between the two organizations, how they're run and how they're perceived by the outside world.

Asked what his impression of the Jets was when he was a Giant, Banks said, "They always had some good talented players, but for the most part they were a group of guys that just didn't know how to win. When you'd looked at them on film, they were almost laughable, but you knew there were always a few players when you played against them that actually did care and would come at you quite hard regardless of how horrible their team was, like [fullback] Brad Baxter. He just came into the game with a chip on his shoulder just to make it interesting.

"The Jets were always second-class citizens in New York," Banks went on. "If we'd all be out in New York

City at the same club, there was tension. You could see those guys had chips on their shoulders any time they were in the same place as us. It never got escalated to a brawl or anything like that, but you couldn't coexist with those guys without evil looks. I really don't think we had an arrogance about us, but any time we ran into those guys, we knew we owned the town.

"It was almost like we'd walk in and they'd see us and say, 'Damn, there goes our night.' We'd run into [running back] Freeman [McNeil] once in a while. Freeman was a good guy, but he wasn't the most sociable guy when Giants were around."

Asked what his impression of the Giants became once he was with the Jets, Banks said he sensed nothing but jealousy from the Jets about the crosstown rival Giants.

"I'll tell you this much, the people in that [Jets] organization, excluding our [Parcells' coaching] staff, hated the Giants," Banks said. "Anything that they could do that was different or better than what the Giants were doing, they wanted to do it. They were bent on being better than the Giants at something. There were some things that were so little, they probably didn't even cross the Giants' radar screen, but those were victories for those guys. Oh, I could see the jealousy."

Banks, though, said that jealousy vibe changed quickly once Parcells set his roots in the organization.

"We didn't feel like second-class citizen as Jets then only because we had Bill Parcells and he was Mr. New

Carl Banks was a member of both New York franchises.

York," Banks said. "So from that end, everyone that worked in the Jets organization who was there before we came in with Bill and his coaching staff had more of a sense of pride than they had in the past.

"I'll tell you this much, the one thing that Bill Parcells brought to that organization that was certainly not there—and I can unequivocally say this—was a sense of pride. He never gave speeches to the non-football staff, but the way he went about his business, he led by example of how things should be run. Everyone in the organization started to walk around with a little more sense of pride and probably didn't feel as much like a second-class citizen the way they did before, because anything Bill said or did made the back pages, something Jim Fassel didn't have."

ANGRY BILL

A year after leaving the Jets, sources who knew of his plans were leaking out that he was going to take over the Tampa Bay Buccaneers in 2001. When a story about his potential return to the NFL appeared in *The New York Post* during Super Bowl week in Tampa, it caused a stir amongst those in the Bucs' organization who knew that the head coach at the time, Tony Dungy, was on shaky ground, having failed to advance the team in the playoffs.

A year later, Bill Parcells was poised to take the Tampa Bay job, just as reported the previous year. Jets offensive line coach Bill Muir took a similar job in Tampa. Then Jets assistant general manager Mike

Tannenbaum was flown to Tampa to interview for the general manager job. The pieces were being put in place for Parcells.

But just as he had in 1992, Parcells got cold feet at the last minute and never took the job, again jilting the Buccaneers.

The following year, he was hired by the Dallas Cowboys after owner Jerry Jones pursued him.

Complicated man, Parcells.

"You think I know Bill Parcells? I don't think anyone knows Bill, even himself," former Giants, Patriots, and Jets running back David Meggett once said.

More than one former player of Parcells has joked, "If Bill was named king of the world on Sunday, he'd be unhappy by Tuesday."

7

CURTIS MARTIN

NEVER IN THE TEAM'S HISTORY has there been a more respected player to walk through the Jets' locker room than Curtis Martin.

Never has there been a tougher player, either, one who was able to will himself onto the field despite having ankle and knee injuries that were severe enough to keep a lesser player out a month.

Martin has always stayed true to his values. A religious man, he's never tried to force-feed anyone his beliefs. He, too, has never said a bad word about anybody—teammate, coach, opponent, anyone.

And all the while, Martin has been perhaps the most consistent productive player to ever wear a Jets uniform.

MARTIN'S BEGINNING

Had it not been for his incredible mother, Rochella, Curtis Martin probably would have died after a wasted youth, never having the chance to achieve in life the way he has.

Martin was a nine-year-old when he and his mother walked into his grandmother's home in Pittsburgh and found her dead lying in bed with a knife stuck though her chest. When Rochella seemed to be losing control of her emotions following the murder, the young Martin looked at her and asked, "If you get sick, who is going to raise me?"

Those words will forever be with Rochella, and they're words that got her together quickly.

"I never wanted anybody to raise my child but me," she told Richard Oliver of *Newsday* in a 1998 interview. "By him saying that, it actually pulled me together. It was the only thing in the world that kept me from losing my sanity."

Martin grew up as what he described as a "knucklehead," running with gangs and breaking the law because he could and because that was the norm. He's spoken openly about being with gangs in the middle of shoot-outs, seeing his friends shot and killed, and wondering why he was never gunned down.

"I thought that the life I was living, in my mind, death was inevitable, just because you see it so much," Martin said in the same *Newsday* interview. "You can be the most innocent person, and it can grab you. All your friends you see get shot, so it's just a matter of time before it happens to you. I used to have these dreams of getting killed a lot of the time. It's almost like in my mind I remember saying one day, 'There has to be more to life than this.'

"My mother always told me, 'Curt, I couldn't handle something else happening to you,'" Martin recalled. "I mean, that is one of the things I can remember clear as yesterday. I would see her, like, ready to just cry because it was like she was worried, 'Is my son going to come back today?'"

With Rochella pushing her son to take up something, anything—even the glee club—Martin went to football, even though he had no initial interest.

Martin ended up gaining more than 2,500 total yards, including 1,705 rushing yards and 20 touchdowns as a senior in 1990. That led to Martin's collegiate career at the University of Pittsburgh, which led to Bill Parcells drafting him in New England.

It was after his senior year the University of Pittsburgh when Martin turned to Christianity and changed his life.

Asked what clicked in his mind to make the drastic life change, Martin said, "I realized that you only get out of life what you put into it."

CREDIT WHERE CREDIT IS DUE

There aren't many—if any—people on earth, other than perhaps his three daughters, who can heighten the emotions of the hardened Bill Parcells the way Curtis Martin has and does.

Martin, the best running back in Jets history, is the son Parcells never had. Never was that evidenced more

than by a poignant incident that occurred in January 2000.

Parcells arrived to his dark corner office upstairs in Weeb Ewbank Hall and found a trophy sitting on his desk with a note attached.

The phone then rang as he settled in his chair. It was his youngest daughter, Jill, who began conversing about something going on in her life when she realized that her father was in a far-off place, nowhere in the vicinity of her conversation.

There was silence on the other end of the phone, and Jill began to worry.

"Dad ...?

Through the receiver, she realized her father was crying.

His sobs were as audible as they were unheard of from this tough, old-school man feared by so many who've crossed his path over the years.

The daughter's immediate reaction was of horror, as if something terrible had happened.

"Dad ...?"

Parcells finally got control of himself, reeling in the emotions and explained to his daughter what had overcome him.

It was Curtis Martin who'd moved Parcells to those uncontrollable tears in the private darkness of his office that day. Before Parcells had gotten to his office, Martin

---

Curtis Martin is a humble man whose outlook has touched many Jets players and fans.

snuck in and made a special delivery, leaving the trophy he'd just won as the team's Most Valuable Player in the 1999 season.

Along with the trophy, Martin left a letter that told Parcells how much he meant to Martin, what kind of father figure he's been to him, and how none of the great things that have happened to Martin would have been possible had it not been for Parcells' care and guidance.

Martin wanted Parcells to know, in no uncertain terms, that the MVP award he was given by his teammates was for Parcells. He wanted Parcells to have the trophy, and he wanted him to know why.

To this day, that trophy remains one of Parcells' most prized possessions. It sits proudly alongside those of the two Super Bowls he led the Giants to in the 1986 and 1990 seasons.

"WHAT ELSE COULD YOU WANT?"

Bill Parcells' ties to Curtis Martin date back to when he drafted Martin out of the University of Pittsburgh in 1995 while he was head coach of the New England Patriots.

When Parcells went to the Jets, he coached in New York for one year before realizing he couldn't live without Martin, and so he orchestrated a complicated deal to sign Martin as an unrestricted free agent, wresting him from the Patriots and making him a Jet.

Since Martin joined the Jets in 1998, he's become one of the top players in the franchise's history, rushing for more than 1,000 yards in each of his six seasons and rushing for 48 touchdowns. For his career, entering the 2004 season, Martin had rushed for 1,000 or more yards in each of his first nine seasons, something only Barry Sanders (10 seasons) has accomplished in NFL history.

"What else could you possibly want out of a player?" Parcells once asked, referring to Martin.

One of the confounding things about Martin is despite his Hall of Fame-like production and his incredible will to stay healthy and play hurt, he's not one of the most recognized or celebrated running backs in the league.

He's not flashy. He's not a walking ESPN SportsCenter sound bite, not a player who jockeys for position for the cameras when they come into the locker room. Martin does not have his own TV or radio show. He does not do guest appearances on the national shows. He doesn't throw parties in his honor during Super Bowl week.

When Martin first moved to Long Island when he became a Jet, he lived like a minimalist for months, in an apartment without a television or much furniture, and he took taxis to work when he wasn't hitching a ride with a teammate.

When Martin was spotted driving an SUV one year, he explained that he'd bought it for his mother, Rochella, but she didn't want it. She wanted him to drive it because she was worried about him.

MARTIN AND RECORDS

Curtis Martin is a most interesting character in that he's not even really a football fan, nor was he as a youth. He said he plays the game so it can help him be able to help others, whether it's financially or spiritually. That has always been what has driven him to be better every year. Martin said he wants his final years in the league to be better and more productive than his early years, something that simply seems an impossibility.

Martin, who in 2004 became only the 15th running back in NFL history to gain 10,000 or more rushing yards, said, "This may sound a little bit ahead of myself, but I want to finish up like Michael Jordan did. He went out on a winning note, on top of his game. Whenever that day comes—maybe five, six years from now when I decide to retire—I want my last year to be better than my first year."

Martin said he wants to "be different" from the other backs who reach the 10,000-yard plateau and see their numbers dwindle as their skills erode.

"There are a lot of boxers who aren't good after a certain number of years," Martin said. "I want to go against the odds. I believe I'll overcome those obstacles that a lot of people don't overcome when they get up in the years in their career. I know how much harder I have to work, how much more on top of my game I have to be."

Martin often harkens back to some of the things Bill Parcells told him when he was younger, and even though he's no longer coached by Parcells, he feeds off those words.

"Parcells said something to me that kind of changed my outlook," Martin said. "He said, 'Son, there's a difference between routine and commitment. Some guys just do a routine over and over again, and some guys are committed to get better.' Sometimes you need someone to speak something like that to you that sparks something new in you. That for me sparked a new flame, a higher flame."

You'll find few players in the league who are as special as Martin.

"Curtis is a low-key dude," Chris Hayes said. "He kind of sparkles in his own way. He's the type of guy who's going to show you instead of talking about it. He's going to prove it to you. The dude is amazing to me. I used to watch him in New England, and I was impressed back then. He's always pushing. Curtis has something special. When he hits that hole, he's full steam and he hits it. He brings a lot of energy and force behind him."

Martin, too, is one of the many professional athletes who has given his life to God as a Christian, but unlike a lot of those same athletes, he doesn't force his beliefs on the outside world. He's a spiritual man who keeps his beliefs to himself unless you want to talk with him about them.

"He's shared some of the things he's been through in his past life, before he came to God," Hayes said. "He's been through a lot, man, and to be where he is now is totally a blessing. He knows that. He's aware of where his gifts come from."

That's why Martin is so giving. That's why he's helped change the lives of so many, including the tough, gruff Bill Parcells.

TUNNEL TRAFFIC

The Jets had just lost to the Kansas City Chiefs on a last-second touchdown at home in 2002, leaving them with a 2-4 record.

As a group of Giants Stadium regular tailgaters, the 16G Crew from Brooklyn, was quietly driving home afterward, John Esposito and Danny Mendez were in the front seat of their van in bumper-to-bumper traffic trying to get through the Lincoln Tunnel.

Both were wearing Curtis Martin jerseys, and the windows were down.

As they waited, a black SUV pulled up alongside of them, and the man inside said to the 16G Crew, "Nice jerseys."

Esposito and Mendez thought he was asking about the game they'd just come from, and both talked about how bad the game was.

The man in the SUV said, "I know. I played in it."

And he then went on to apologize for the game.

Curtis Martin was apologizing for his team's performance and offering encouraging words like, "Don't worry. We're going to rally."

Martin then, through his window, signed hats, shirts, and whatever else Esposito, Mendez, Patricia

Hankin, and Warren Flagg handed to him, before saying, "Thanks for your support."

He then drove off into the tunnel.

HUMBLE HERO

After all these years of incredible athletic and personal accomplishment, when Curtis Martin thinks back to those days and reflects on the incredible path he's followed since, he says the fortune he's encountered "humbles" him.

"It's one of the most humbling reflections that I have, because I look at things and I say, 'Why me? Who am I? ... Someone so bad and so contrary to what's right, to end up in a situation like this?'" Martin said. "It makes me so grateful. That's why I tell people it's hard for me to be bigheaded or arrogant about anything, because it definitely wasn't in my plans to be in this situation. I was just taking it a step at a time and I ended up here."

Martin has forged a Hall of Fame career here and helped elevate a franchise that had been devoid of a top running back since the retirement of Freeman McNeil. To illustrate the kind of company he keeps in the NFL record books, during the 2003 season, Martin surpassed O.J. Simpson to move into 12th place on the NFL's rushing list.

"It's a lie to say it doesn't mean anything," Martin said of the milestone. "I definitely wouldn't have imagined anything like this, but it's become a reality now."

The shrewd and intricate maneuver by Bill Parcells to wrest Martin away from the Patriots as a restricted free agent before the 1998 season will go down as one of the great transactions in NFL history.

The fact that Martin ended up in New York, a place he vowed never to come to, makes his story even more compelling.

"This used to be a place I hated the most," Martin said. "I used to say, 'I'll never live in New York.' Now it's a place I never want to leave. Who would have known I would have loved playing for the New York Jets? I wasn't a big football fan, but one thing I used to say was, 'I never want to play for the New York Jets; I never want to be on that team,' because I always felt the New York Jets were the worst team in the NFL."

Herman Edwards, who's very close with Martin, said people won't realize his low-key star's greatness "probably until he walks up there and gets inducted to the Hall of Fame."

8

BILL BELICHICK

LOSING IS SOMETHING the Jets have been quite proficient at in their star-crossed history. The loss they suffered on January 4, 2000, though, is yet another off-field gaffe in the Jets' distressing lore.

Upon the drama of Bill Parcells' ballyhooed exit from coaching, the Jets were going to make everything right by elevating Bill Belichick, Parcells' top lieutenant and architect of his Super Bowl defenses, to take over as the 12th head coach in Jets history.

Belichick, though, suddenly had other plans, and those plans included not losing a single game as the Jets' head coach.

As Parcells' retirement from coaching unfolded amidst an imminent team ownership change, Belichick, already a onetime loser as a head coach in Cleveland, where he never really had a chance to succeed because of a litany of outside influences, realized the Jets might end up being his black hole if he didn't escape.

Bill Belichick turned the press conference announcing his ascension to head coach into a rambling resignation speech.

Two-time losers as head coaches almost never get a third chance, so Belichick was wary of another failure with the strong hand of Parcells still ruling the organization and a new owner about to take over for more than $600 million.

It didn't hurt Belichick that the New England Patriots, a Jets nemesis, had been sniffing around regarding his services if he could wrest himself from the grips of Parcells and the Jets. Patriots owner and Parcells nemesis Robert Kraft, in his own clandestine way, had gotten word to Belichick through intermediaries that if he could break free from the Jets, the Patriots would give him complete control of all personnel moves as their head coach, not to mention about $2 million per year.

So what transpired on January 4, 2000, was one of the most bizarre press conferences in the history of sports.

H.C. OF THE N.Y.J.

With a full house of reporters and television cameras assembled in the auditorium of Weeb Ewbank Hall—the same place where the late owner Leon Hess had introduced Rich Kotite with the infamous words, "I'm 80 years old, and I want results now"—Bill Belichick resigned when he was supposed to be announced as the new head coach of the organization.

In unquestionably one of the most embarrassing days for the franchise, a disheveled and uncomfortable Belichick, in a rambling 25-minute opening statement, announced that he was resigning.

Moments before he entered the auditorium, Belichick had marched into the office of Jets president Steve Gutman and handed him his resignation letter, which was a handwritten note scrawled on a crumpled piece of paper, stating on it that he was resigning "as h.c. of the n.y.j."

"I feel like I'm making a decision based on circumstances and the situation as it is right now," Belichick said. "The agreement that I made was with Mr. Hess, Bill Parcells, and Mr. Gutman and that situation has changed dramatically, and it's going to change even further. There's going to be some point in time in the near future where the head coach would not be talking to John Hess and they may not be talking to Steve Gutman and we know they may not be speaking to Bill Parcells.

"If I'm letting anybody down, I'm sorry, but the situation has changed, and I have to do what's fair to everybody involved."

THE FALLOUT

Jets players were flabbergasted by the latest calamity to engulf the franchise.

"Not that the situation is funny, but it is kind of funny," cornerback Aaron Glenn said. "I think everyone has to wonder about themselves. A new owner is coming in now, and no one knows what's going to happen. I don't think much stuff is crazy, but this is about the craziest thing I've seen."

Receiver Keyshawn Johnson, who was distraught enough about Bill Parcells leaving, said, "Here we go again with some type of uncertainty within the organization. I'm looking at, I guess, my fourth head coach in four years. It kind of makes you wonder what's up with your future."

The newspaper headline writers were rather unkind to Bill Belichick at the time, with *The New York Post* reading: "Belichicken: Jets Better off without Quitter." Another headline read: "Belichick Arnold."

Steve Gutman, then the team president who had overseen a staggering amount of losing during his time in charge of the franchise, unleashed what could only be described as an irresponsible, slanderous character assassination of Belichick in an obvious effort to save face. After Belichick's rambling press conference, the disheveled Belichick left the room and Gutman, dressed sharply in his usual conservative suit, began a barrage attack of damage control by bad-mouthing Belichick. He took advantage of the group of reporters in the room crowded around him to try to paint a desperate picture of Belichick while attempting to sell the fact that the Jets' management was still very much in control.

"Bill's conversation certainly tells me we should have some feelings of sorrow and regret for him and his family as he's obviously in some turmoil, and I have to wish him the best with whatever the future holds for him," Gutman said. "I'm not a psychologist, but I think I just listened for an hour to a person who is in some turmoil and deserves our understanding and our consideration."

Those words, unfounded and to the point of slanderous, would later come back to haunt Gutman.

CHAOS

Carl Banks, who'd been on Bill Parcells' staff and who played for both Parcells and Bill Belichick, said he'll never forget that day Belichick suddenly stepped down as head coach the day he was to be hired.

Banks walked into a quiet weight room that morning and found Belichick, by himself, running on the treadmill. Still under the impression that Belichick was Parcells' successor as the Jets' head coach, Banks asked him if there was anything he needed to help get ready for the press conference to announce his elevation to head coach.

"No, Carl. Thanks. I'll be fine," Belichick said.

About two hours later, Belichick went public with his shocking news.

"You've got to give him credit, because he was his own man, and a lot of coaches would have never stepped down on faith to say, 'OK, I'm not working in the shadow. I've got to blaze my own trail,'" Banks said.

Upstairs, Parcells was seething after Belichick informed him of his decision. For Parcells, the ultimate control freak, the plan he had orchestrated down to the last detail was suddenly out of his control, and that made him livid.

"Parcells was angry," Banks recalled. "That was the best word to describe it. Bill Parcells is a guy who does a lot for a lot of people. You'll never hear about it, but he puts a premium on helping people. He tries to help people that help him. He and Belichick had this relationship that was this whole Oscar-Felix thing for a while, but it probably shocked the hell out of Parcells because it wasn't discussed.

"In Parcells' mind, he said, 'Bill's a guy that deserves to be a head coach, and I'm going to give him the opportunity right here.' Bill had his own way. He's not going to come up and hug you and kiss you on the cheek and say, 'Hey, buddy, I love you, and I'm going to make you my next head coach.' It was kind of unspoken in saying, 'You're the next guy.'

"But in the end, it was one of those deals where Belichick did his own soul searching and decided he didn't want to do it. There were things about the organization that Belichick didn't like."

REVENGE

In the end, after the unrest and innuendo that followed his decision not to take over as the Jets' head coach when Bill Parcells quit, Bill Belichick got his revenge, winning a court battle with the team to release him from his contract and taking over as the New England Patriots' head coach and winning two Super Bowls.

Meanwhile, Steve Gutman, who was known essentially as a caddie for Leon Hess, opening car doors for him and shielding him from reporters and the public, was phased out of the organization (not without an absurd $4.75 million golden parachute) once the new ownership arrived.

Belichick went on and found resounding success in New England, building the Patriots into what many term "the model franchise."

In a quiet moment in the days leading up to the 2004 AFC championship game, Belichick was asked about those ridiculous statements that Gutman had made four years earlier. He'd never spoken publicly about what went down that day, particularly about Gutman's unfounded assessment of his mental state.

"I'm going to make one comment, and we can close the book on it," Belichick said. "I can't think of anybody in professional sports—and certainly in my 30 years of professional football—who has said more and won less than Steve Gutman."

Belichick, too, noted that all of the uncertainties that surrounded the franchise at the time of his resignation ended up coming to fruition.

"I knew I did the right thing, and I didn't know where my career was going to go," Belichick said. "I knew what wasn't going to happen. All the things I said then, frankly, they've all come true. Every aspect of the organization that I commented on, it looks to me like that's the way I saw it then and that's the way it turned out."

9

AL GROH

AT LEAST AL GROH'S TENURE as the Jets' head coach lasted longer than Bill Belichick's.

His legacy, however, is about as invisible as any head coach in Jets history, because it was sandwiched between the end of Bill Parcells' three eventful years and the beginning of the Herman Edwards era. Groh's 9-7 playoff-less season seems to be less than a blip on the radar in team history. Nothing really remarkable happened with Groh at the helm either.

Groh's downfall in the end, before he bolted to the serenity and security of his alma mater, the University of Virginia, was that he tried to become Parcells rather than trying to simply be himself. Groh's tough-guy act grew old with the players, who began to see through it and resent it.

It seemed that Groh, too, became tired of the rigors of being a head coach in the NFL. He entered the job as a very amicable man with reporters, always with an

intelligent and pithy analysis, analogy, or story, and he left beleaguered and seemingly beaten down by the relentless volume of media he had to deal with on a daily basis.

Groh's sudden departure to Virginia was his escape from life under the strong thumb of Bill Parcells. Groh, like many of the minions who've worked for Parcells, always found himself mired in a catch-22 because with Parcells they often were successful and well paid, but at the same time they were demeaned by his management style, which included muzzling them around reporters.

Groh's departure came just six days after his team missed the playoffs by losing 34-20 to the Ravens in Baltimore, ending a season that began with six wins in the first seven games and a 9-4 record before losing the final three games to miss the playoffs. It would mean a fourth head coach since the previous January if you include Bill Belichick's don't-blink tenure.

A KEY TRADE

Before Al Groh would even coach a game, on April 11, 2000, the unthinkable and unimaginable occurred. The Jets traded away their franchise player, dynamic receiver Keyshawn Johnson.

The move was controversial for a number of reasons, beginning with the fact that Johnson was the Jets' most explosive offensive weapon. Add in the fact that Johnson's threats to hold out for a restructured

Al Groh tried Bill Parcells' tough-guy approach, but the players never accepted him as the reason they won.

contract for a large raise scared the Jets as well as the fact that Johnson never really got along with Groh.

The upshot for the Jets in the deal were two first-round draft picks from the Tampa Bay Buccaneers in the trade, picks that turned out to be defensive end John Abraham and tight end Anthony Becht.

Still, though, the trade left Jets fans infuriated, particularly with Johnson, who in his typical way chirped about how Groh ran him out of town and naïvely exonerated Bill Parcells, who was the team's director of football operations at the time.

Groh called the decision to deal Johnson "a unanimous decision among all the major decision makers" on the team, adding that it was about "all financial considerations," not personal as Johnson claimed it was.

"Do you think we traded the player because I don't think he's a good player?" Groh asked at the time. "Do you think I made the trade to make me more popular? Don't you think I want to win? When the obituaries are written, there's going to be only one person who has the Jets' won-lost record in his obit—me."

As much as Johnson wanted to make it all about Groh making the decision, Groh said, "It wasn't a unilateral decision. A lot of good minds met for many hours on this. This was a 'we' decision. I was probably the last one to cast my vote."

Groh consulted trusted assistant Maurice Carthon before making the move. Carthon, a former NFL fullback, told Groh that with or without Johnson, the

Jets would have a good team and advised him to trade him if he thought the receiver would be a distraction.

At it turned out, the Jets finished 9-7 and out of the playoffs in 2000 without Johnson.

Many people around the NFL believed that the Jets ran scared of Johnson's contract demands when they really held the hammer all along.

"Here's one case where everyone would benefit from the formula of [the late Giants general manager] George Young," a high-ranking NFL official told *The New York Post*. "I don't think George Young would deal a guy like that. If George Young were handling this, he'd know [Johnson's threats] were just rhetoric, and he'd know the strength of the player. I don't think George Young would throw the baby out with the bath water. Johnson is their biggest producer. They could be crippling their team."

One prominent NFL agent said after the deal was made he spoke to a Buccaneers front office person who said, "I cannot believe [the Jets] are making this trade. I am shocked that we're getting this deal done. I can't believe [the Jets] are doing this."

Neither could Jets fans, who were forced to digest yet another helping of calamity.

A SOUR REACTION

Keyshawn Johnson never thought the Jets would call his bluff and he surely didn't want to leave New York, which explained his negative reaction when the Jets finally made the move.

"I could see where the fans would be a little disappointed," Johnson said. "New York sports fans are some of the best sports fans in the world if not the best. I had a joyful career with them my first four years, and I was excited every single game to come out of that tunnel [at Giants Stadium] and see those guys screaming and hollering. I tried to fill them with plenty of memories and things of that nature."

The shocking trade of Johnson left the Jets' organization reeling once again. At the time of his trade, in a span of four months, the Jets lost Parcells, a Hall of Fame-bound head coach; Bill Belichick, his hand-picked successor who bolted for New England; several members of their top assistant coaching staff such as Charlie Weis; and then Johnson, their best player.

"To lose Keyshawn, Bill Belichick, Bill Parcells, and most of the coaching staff, it's going to be tough to recover from that," Jets cornerback Otis Smith said at the time. "Hopefully, the coaching staff we have now can do a good job, although that remains to be seen. We have a lot of work ahead of us. To lose one of your best players ... wow, it's a tough loss ... a huge loss."

A YEAR IN FLUX

The Al Groh era began with a 20-16 win over the Packers in Green Bay, and it offered such promise to the future from his new regime. A week later, Groh's Jets beat New England to go 2-0 and left Bill Belichick's Patriots 0-2. There was joy in Jetsville, with everyone in

Vinny Testaverde (16) and Curtis Martin (28) led the team during the Al Groh tenure.

the building sure the right decisions had been made with regard to the coaching fiasco months earlier.

On October 23, 2000, the Jets went into their home locker room at halftime being blown out and embarrassed by Miami on the *Monday Night Football* national stage, and Groh had steam coming out of his ears. Inside the locker room, where some furniture was thrown around, Groh screamed at his players, challenging their pride.

Something clicked, because the Jets would come out in the second half and engineer one of the greatest comebacks in NFL history, overcoming a 23-point deficit in the fourth quarter to win 40-37 in overtime in what was immediately dubbed, "The Monday Night Miracle." The Jets tied the game on a Vinny Testaverde play-action fake pass to 325-pound tackle Jumbo Elliott, who made a diving catch in the end zone. That was a highlight of the Groh era, one that would unfortunately end without a playoff berth.

BLOWN OPPORTUNITY

Oakland would continue to be the bane of the Jets' existence in 2000, this time with Al Groh coaching. In this game, the Jets marched into Oakland with a 9-4 record, needing only one win in their final three to advance to the playoffs. With a win over the Raiders, the Jets would have had sole possession of first place in the AFC East and control of their own destiny in hand.

That's what made their embarrassing 31-7 loss to the Raiders so curious. When it was over, the Jets looked completely downtrodden as they slowly dressed in front of their locker stalls inside the visitor's locker room. There wasn't a lot of anger in the room. It was more a sense of complete disappointment in themselves, players knowing they let themselves down as well as their fans.

"We blew it," Jets running back Curtis Martin said. "We blew an opportunity. That's the worst we've played all year and probably since I've been here."

Added Jets linebacker Roman Phifer: "We had everything laid out for us. All we had to do was do our part."

ANOTHER MOTOWN MOMENT

In 2000, there was yet another Detroit debacle to further haunt the Jets' existence. It was another playoff-busting moment.

With two games to play, a 9-5 record, and the Jets hosting the Lions at Giants Stadium, one win in the final two games would assure Al Groh of bringing the Jets to the playoffs in his first season as an NFL head coach.

But with 12 seconds remaining in a game that had no business being so close, Jets kicker John Hall was wide left with a 35-yard field goal attempt that would have tied the game at 10-10. The miss, a low, ugly one, left the Jets with a 10-7 loss. The Jets seemed to be exasperated to even be in the position of tying the game given that they were playing at home and favored to beat the Lions, seemingly a lesser team. So when Hall's field goal attempt missed, there was shock amongst the players as the reality of the loss set in. This was yet another blown chance for them.

Hall, as he always was in the face of adversity, was stand-up about his miss, saying, "I just need another chance. I feel next week can't get here quick enough."

What no one realized at the time was that next week would not come for Hall, who was left at home for the Jets' season finale in Baltimore. Groh, never a big fan of Hall, was so angry about his miss against Detroit that he signed free agent kicker Brett Conway and brought him to Baltimore instead of Hall. It seemed to be the end of his career as a Jet.

FERGIE RIPS GROH

Jason Ferguson, a starting nose tackle who was to enter the 2001 off-season as a free agent, snapped before reporters, telling them he would never come back to play for Al Groh. This was the day after the 2000 season ended with players cleaning out their lockers and getting into their running cars on the parking lot to bolt for the off-season. Ferguson had just packed his belongings into a couple of large green garbage bags when a couple of reporters approached him to talk about the disappointing season and his future. This, Ferguson figured, was the perfect time to unload his pent-up feelings.

"I think this is my last year," Ferguson said. "When you have a situation where your boss has a grudge over you, you've got to look at it as it's time for me to start over. It's time for me to start over. I'm going to start over."

Groh had replaced Ferguson with Ernie Logan in the starting lineup after a game against the Bears, saying that Logan earned his way onto the field by forcing opponents' fumbles in consecutive games. Ferguson at the time conceded that he made some poor plays in the loss to the Bears, but he still felt like he was being made a scapegoat for the loss.

"I haven't said anything [to Groh] since," Ferguson said. "We ain't never been eye to eye since I've been

Jason Ferguson (far right) disliked Al Groh so much that he said he would leave the Jets. Groh left two weeks later, and Ferguson stayed with the team.

here. That started when I came here in 1997. We never got along. I can't single out one thing, but when it's you and him in the hallway and you don't speak to him and he don't speak to you, you figure out those things on your own. Then he became the head coach, and right then I knew I was up shit creek.

"I don't think I would have a chance to be happy if I stayed," Ferguson went on. "If you're not having fun and you play with injuries and then you're faced with a boss that you really can't stand looking at ... he feels the same way about me. It's cool. It's a business. He plays the players he likes. There's no doubt I'd love to play here, but when you've got things happening like what happened to me this year, like him calling me a lazy player, I know it's time to start over."

Much to Ferguson's—and everyone else's—surprise, Groh stepped down just weeks after Ferguson's pledge to not return, and Ferguson was re-signed later in the off-season.

MAWAE'S PARTING SHOTS

Al Groh's departure spurred Jets center Kevin Mawae to voice his displeasure with this former head coach.

Mawae, speaking to Rich Cimini of the *Daily News*, ripped Groh almost as soon as Groh had cleared his office, ranting about how players were delighted that he was leaving.

"I don't think there's much heartache about Al leaving," Mawae said. "Guys aren't hurt that he's gone.

For the most part, guys weren't happy. It's hard to play for a guy when you're not happy. It went from star guys all the way down to the practice squad. We always talked about having high-character guys in the locker room; that's what held the team together. The team leaders did a good job. Yeah, we were 6-1 at one point, but a lot of that was despite the fact that Al was the coach. That was the feeling on the team.

"He tried to micromanage, and a lot of guys tuned him out a long time ago."

Mawae was angered by the fact that Groh didn't have any sort of caste system, where veterans got to take it easy in some cases to save their bodies.

"We did one-on-one pass-rushing drills, and they ended up being a full-blown deal with no pads," Mawae complained. "It got to a point where it was a little out of control. Somebody went to talk to Al, and he was like, 'It's hard to do it any other way, isn't it?' I thought to myself, 'You can't do this. You're going to kill the team.' A lot of guys felt, 'If it ain't broken, don't fix it.' There wasn't a lot of love lost."

Groh, days later, shot back at Mawae's complaints, saying, "Mawae was always one of the guys who didn't want to work. He was one of those guys where he didn't have to say it, but he was one of the players who didn't want to work. He always worked hard, but I knew that he was one of the players who wished that it was the other way around.

"Look, I don't want to get into a point-counterpoint in the press. But one of the things you have to do to be the coach is you can't care what people say about you. So it doesn't bother me when they say that stuff about practices. I thought we needed a physically and mentally tough team that proved that it would endure through very challenging circumstances. I'm not talking about being a jackass about killing players in practice. But you don't become a tough-minded, physically tough team by just fooling around."

SHOCK AND MORE UNCERTAINTY

Jets cornerback Ray Mickens remembered returning home to find his answering machine tied up with some 15 messages when Al Groh suddenly resigned.

He recalled thinking, "This is crazy. It's ridiculous. It caught me off guard. I don't think this has ever happened that two coaches have quit in a matter of a year. Al did a good job for us. I guess he saw an opportunity to be a coach at his alma mater. I guess it's more secure and less stress being in college.

"It was a shock. It leaves a lot of uncertainty. You definitely want to have a coach and know exactly what you've got to do."

Mickens said he immediately hoped Bill Parcells would return to the sideline, "He's the best coach I ever played for. You'd love to have somebody like that back. But his desires may be somewhere else."

As history has told us, they seemingly always are.

10

KEY AND Q

THEIR LOCKERS were right next to each other. Keyshawn Johnson and Wayne Chrebet. Both receivers. Both teammates. Credit Clay Hampton, then the assistant equipment manager, for putting together one of the most entertaining neighboring locker combinations in NFL history.

They were two players who couldn't stand each other. They were two teammates who detested the very being of one another. One was from the bright lights of Los Angeles, and the other from the dreary streets of Garfield, New Jersey. One was a No. 1 overall draft pick out of USC. The other was an undrafted free agent out of Hofstra University, who played college ball right across the street from the Jets' training facility. One was an instant millionaire. The other drove the same broken-down car for the first couple years of his NFL career.

Who of the two was the most real, the most sincere, and the guy you'd most want to hang out with?

Initially, Chrebet seemed to have the edge, but mostly because of the book, the one Johnson coauthored with *Sports Illustrated* writer Shelley Smith, who used to baby-sit him in L.A. Johnson made some derogatory statements about Chrebet's receiving skills, along with a litany of other rather humorous assessments about the 1-15 team he played on his rookie year.

Difficult as it may have been for some to accept, a lot of what Johnson wrote was cold, hard truth, the kind that the politically correct set shy away from as if they were being audited by the IRS.

Johnson called Chrebet, the underdog 10th man on the depth chart who made good, nothing more than a team "mascot." But what Chrebet had accomplished to that point—albeit on losing teams—was too impressive to be passed off with that kind of statement. Chrebet had 84 receptions to Johnson's 63 in 1996.

"We need a quarterback who isn't afraid to throw down the field, someone who just doesn't dump off four- and five-yard passes when we need seven for a first down, someone who won't throw everything to the coach's pet," Johnson said in his book, referring to Chrebet.

Chrebet, who was given the nickname "Q" by linebacker Bobby Houston because so many players in the locker room mispronounced his last name, always took the high road in the Johnson flap, smartly playing off of the character that the media built him as—the underdog, the little guy who made it in the big guys' world.

COEXISTENCE

Wayne Chrebet and Keyshawn Johnson continued to coexist for years without speaking to each other despite dressing alongside one another every day. Johnson's big-time attitude and his book, *Give Me the Damn Ball*, were enough to turn Chrebet off for good.

"I don't know what's on his mind," Chrebet said. "I think he should just take care of his business like the rest of us. Off the field, there's no relationship, that's obvious, nor will there be a chance of one now. I'm bigger than that, to sink down to his level. He can do whatever he wants to sell his book, but I'm here to win games. That's all that's important right now, and that's what he should be thinking about."

Johnson reasoned, "You don't have to have a relationship with the players off the field. You're a team on the field. You're a team in the coaching staff room when you're watching films. When you go home, they're going to their house."

Former teammate and fellow receiver Dedric Ward once said of the two, "I don't know what kind of relationship they carry off the field, but on the field, it's definitely a business manner. In the huddle, when we're all in there together, we talk about and discuss what's going on, congratulate each other on the big catch. You wouldn't be able to tell they have problems off the field, because they act like best friends on the field."

That's where it ends, though, and there was no denying that by Chrebet.

"There is no past," Chrebet said. "We didn't like each other from the start. People still don't understand that it had nothing to do with the book. We just didn't like each other. It's the same as it was when he initially came in, just from minicamp as a rookie, a young kid coming in trying to throw his weight around. We didn't get along from the start. On the field, all that matters is what we're doing out there."

THE BOOK

Many Jets were very agitated by Keyshawn Johnson's book, even their legendary former quarterback Joe Namath, who weighed in on the book, saying, "He's got to understand he's wrong. Until Keyshawn can accept the fact that he could be wrong or that he is wrong at times, he's going to have a struggle. I've never approved of talk going outside the framework of the team, from Beaver Falls, Pennsylvania, to Alabama to the New York Jets. That's the way I was taught; that's the way I believe. I don't believe anything constructive is going to come from getting outside your work area.

"Talking about how Wayne Chrebet would not be able to play somewhere else, that's downright ignorant. Hopefully, the players will be able to get through to him. You've got to learn that with the guys you live with—until that stuff gets squared away, it's going to be a distraction. I don't know if Wayne and Keyshawn are talking at all. It would seem that Wayne is owed an apology, and Keyshawn would be man enough to say, 'Hey, I made a mistake. This cat can play.'"

Johnson's response to the possibility that he might have made a mistake regarding Chrebet: "No, not at all. If it was a mistake, I wouldn't have written my book."

WILL THE REAL CHREBET PLEASE STAND UP?

Wayne Chrebet has been one of the most confounding players to pass through the Jets' locker room.

His background is well documented. He came out of Garfield, a blue-collar town in North Jersey and went to Hofstra University, which, of course, happens to be where the Jets train. Chrebet set and broke numerous records at Hofstra and, as expected, went undrafted and was signed as a free agent by the Jets.

At first, he was perceived to be one of those too-good-to-be-true, feel-good stories about the local kid trying to make the big-time pro team in his home city. When training camp began, Chrebet was last on a depth chart that ran 11 deep at receiver. Fortunately for him, he was trying to break in on a very bad football team, coached by Rich Kotite.

Chrebet, of course, made it, becoming the Jets' leading receiver in 1995, his rookie season.

The thing about Chrebet is that he's a remarkable talent and has an incredible story as one who came from

nowhere to make a name for himself in the NFL. He was no charity case. He was the best receiver the Jets had in training camp that summer, and he'll forever be the most positive thing to come out of the Kotite era. Kotite brought him into the league and believed in him, and he should be credited for that, because a lot of other coaches would have looked at Chrebet's size and speed figures and not even given him a chance.

As Chrebet established himself as one of the best players on the team and one of the league's better receivers, the media deified him as the little guy that could, the small-town kid who made it in New York, and the man with the never-say-die work ethic.

When Keyshawn Johnson arrived, wrote his book, and ridiculed Chrebet, the natural reaction was to side with Chrebet, the underdog, and scoff at Johnson, the No. 1 draft pick with the millions of dollars and the ego the size of the Los Angeles Coliseum.

Johnson was an easy target because of his immature rants in the book. Chrebet, meanwhile, quietly played up his underdog status.

POTENT TANDEM

For all of their disdain for each other, Keyshawn Johnson and Wayne Chrebet were a very good tandem of starting receivers. On the field, Chrebet and Johnson excelled together. In Johnson's second season in 1997,

On the field Keyshawn Johnson (19) and Wayne Chrebet (80) were on the same team, but off the field they detested each other and it was every man for himself.

Johnson had 70 catches and Chrebet 58. In 1998, they enjoyed their best seasons together, with Johnson catching 83 passes and scoring 10 touchdowns and Chrebet hauling in 75 passes and scoring eight touchdowns.

"All people know is, 'Oh, there's tension on the team,' that's the angle they look for," Johnson said. "You don't necessarily have to be best friends. We're two different personalities. I think Wayne really understood where I was coming from [regarding the book]. Whether he read the book, I don't know, but I think he understood.

"He's always painted as a guy in blue jeans and T-shirt, and all I do is sit around in thousand-dollar courtside seats at Knicks games. It's not my fault that guys come to me and ask me if I want to sit at Knicks-Lakers games. I wear jeans, and I wear T-shirts. I grew up totally different than he did, but I'm pretty sure he likes basketball, too."

Glenn Foley, a backup quarterback for the Jets in the late 1990s, said of the odd couple receivers, "They're true professionals, unbelievable in every aspect of the game. When you watch them block, they have to be the best blocking receivers in the league."

Bill Parcells, who inherited Johnson and his book mess, typically took a pragmatic approach.

"If he makes plays, they'll like him," Parcells said. "And if he doesn't make plays, they won't like him."

NUMBER 80

Before that 1998 season, NFL Films asked Wayne Chrebet Sr. for any old film footage of the family for a TV special they were doing on his son. He broke out a tin of film he'd never once viewed in 31 years and gave it to them. It was tape of an interview Eyewitness News had taken of Wayne Sr. in a hospital in Vietnam.

Wayne Jr. never even knew about it and hadn't seen it until the feature was debuted at the Supper Club in Manhattan. The Wayne Chrebet with the Purple Heart at age 19 is such a dead ringer for the Wayne who wears No. 80 that looking at it sends chills down your spine. As the son watched his father on that reel of film tears filled his eyes, completely defying the stoic manner he often displays in public. Wayne Chrebet Jr., who already had a deep appreciation and respect for his father, had taken this to another level, one that surprised him at his reaction.

Wayne Chrebet Sr. had never spoken to his son about what occurred in Vietnam and, the father said, "He's never asked me about it, because he doesn't want to cause me any pain."

Chrebet recalled when he and his then-girlfriend, now-wife, Amy, watched *Saving Private Ryan* together and he couldn't get out of the theater fast enough to go thank his father.

ENIGMATIC WAYNE

When you sit with Wayne Chrebet one on one, he isn't a bad guy. He is, in fact, a good guy.

In a *New York Post* interview with him before the Jets were to play the Jacksonville Jaguars in the playoffs in the 1998 season, Chrebet revealed a special side of himself, his undying devotion to his family.

"My family has never been father-son-mother-daughter," Chrebet said of his parents, Wayne Sr. and Paulette, and his sister, Jennifer. "It's been four best friends since me and my sister grew to be adults."

Chrebet's parents, since the moment he entered the league as that long-shot free agent, have always traveled to virtually every road game.

"At first, I was like ... I didn't feel silly, but I'm a grown man and my parents came to all the games," Chrebet said. "I mean, my father still wears my jersey. That's just how proud he is. I finally understood I must be the luckiest person in the world to still have family that's that interested in what I do."

When Chrebet went to a Super Bowl for the first time as a fan, in 1996, he took his father, saying, "I took my father because he's my best friend."

Chrebet revealed in that interview that he'd written his sister a six-page letter titled, "Ghosts of Christmas Past, Ghosts of Christmas Present, Ghosts of Christmas Future," with a special message at the end of it.

"It was Christmas Day before he left for practice," Jennifer Chrebet recalled. "He wanted me to read it out loud with the four of us sitting together. While I was reading it, I was thinking, 'Wow, how many frames do I need?' Because I wanted to frame every page. The letter was completely priceless. To me, this was the present."

But there was more. On the last page, Chrebet wrote to his sister that he was going to buy her a house.

"Whatever house she wants," Chrebet said. "I haven't even bought myself a house yet, but that's how much I love my sister. Besides winning championships, which is all I want for myself, everything else is for my family."

Chrebet's father, describing the scene at the Chrebet's home, said, "We were all sitting on the couch crying."

"Being around Wayne makes you a better person," the elder Chrebet said. "Being around Wayne brings you up to another level. I don't know why. I can't explain it. But the way he is makes you try to harder to be a better person."

HOLLYWOOD ENDING FOR JERSEY GUY

The sting from Keyshawn Johnson's book quietly wore away thanks mostly to the success Bill Parcells brought to the perennial losing franchise. That didn't mean there was any thaw in the Wayne Chrebet-Johnson relationship, which remained as icy as ever—right through the day Johnson was traded away to the Tampa Bay Buccaneers after the 1999 season.

The feud made a meeting between the Jets and Buccaneers in Tampa Bay in 2000 as spicy as it gets between two teams that rarely face each other.

Johnson, in an interview with Dave Hutchinson from the Newark (New Jersey) *Star-Ledger* several days

Wayne Chrebet catches his breath after nabbing the game-winning touchdown against Keyshawn Johnson's Tampa Bay Buccaneers.

before the anticipated matchup, couldn't resist lobbing a few grenades.

His primary target was Chrebet.

"You're trying to compare a flashlight to a star," Johnson said, of course referring to Chrebet as the flashlight and himself as the star. "Flashlights only last so long. A star is in the sky forever.

"A lot of guys played with me, so they've got a lot to prove to me, I've got nothing to prove against them," Johnson said of the Jets before the game. "They're trying to prove to me that they don't need me. They're trying to prove to me, that since I'm not there, they're better. They say it's not affecting them, then it's not affecting them.

"I know every [bleeping] thing that they do," Johnson rambled on. "Ha! They lost more than a football player in me. They lost a personality, a fun-loving person. And I know that. I know because I talk to them every day and they tell me that."

Johnson had no idea at the time how long the legs of those comments would turn out to be and how he'd later be trampled by them.

What happened that game between the Jets and Bucs simply could not have been written any better for the Jets if the script of the game was predetermined.

Chrebet caught the winning touchdown pass, on a dramatic halfback option pass from running back Curtis Martin with 52 seconds remaining in the game. Johnson caught one pass—a shovel pass that was more like a running play—gaining a mere yard.

"I can't explain it," Johnson said of his anemic production that night. "How can I explain it? That's the plays we called and we ran them efficiently and we ran the ball well. We didn't throw the ball all that well."

Despite taking the so-called high road, Chrebet's expression could hardly hide his glee at showing up Johnson. There was certainly more to Chrebet's emotions than what came out of his words.

"I can stand up here and I could say things and point fingers and this and that," Chrebet said after the game. "But I'm bigger than that. I'm not going to do that. I'm happy for myself and I'm happy for my team and the coaching staff that we're 4-0."

The day after the game, Johnson was still trying to play it cool, as if watching his nemesis catch the game-winning touchdown didn't bother him in the least.

"So, you want to get me? You want to shut up the loudmouth kid from the ghetto? So what?" Johnson said. "That's not going to do it. You're not going to humble me. That's not going to make me regret doing anything."

FLASHLIGHTS FLICKER AND BEAM

What occurred following the dramatic Jets comeback win over the Buccaneers was pure theater.

Playing off of Keyshawn Johnson's flashlight comments about Wayne Chrebet, Al Groh handed out flashlights to his players during his team meeting with the players. He then had players from each unit on the team turn them on during a meeting until the entire room was lighted.

"Any one of these single flashlights in a darkened room is obviously not enough to illuminate the room," Groh would explain later. "A few more illuminated the room somewhat, but it was probably not bright enough to get the job done. Out of the darkness came plenty of light to operate. As long as we all have our lights on, we're in business."

Groh was always a metaphor man. And the players genuinely rallied around this stunt—at least for a while.

There were, indeed, flashlights in players' lockers for their next game, against the Pittsburgh Steelers at Giants Stadium.

Either the batteries ran out or the bulbs burnt out from Tampa Bay to New Jersey, because the Jets failed to find their way out of the day and were waxed by the Steelers 20-3.

A CHANGED CHREBET

Once Keyshawn Johnson was out of his hair and Wayne Chrebet was more established on the team, a different side of him began to surface.

In 2001, with the Jets' offense struggling and Chrebet out of the lineup with an injury, he watched a Jets road loss from his New Jersey home with his wife and some of her friends. A couple days after the game, Chrebet, clearly taking a shot at offensive coordinator Paul Hackett's conservative offense, said that his wife and her friends were calling out what running play the Jets were going to run before it would unfold before their eyes on the TV set.

When reporters wrote about Chrebet's account of the incident, Chrebet realized the heat he'd created inside the organization and, of course, blamed the messengers. That began a boycott of reporters by Chrebet, who blamed them with the age-old player excuse, taking his comments out of context and blowing the situation out of proportion.

In the 2002 season, Chrebet was at it again, seemingly creating a media frenzy and then going into hiding.

Chrebet, by his own volition and not being provoked by a reporter's questions, lashed out at

Hackett in a *New York Times* story, telling the reporter, Judy Battista, that he and Hackett had no relationship whatsoever and strongly indicating that Hackett was simply ignoring him in the offense. Oh, and by the way, Chrebet's comments came with the team in the midst of a three-game winning streak, making the supposed underdog team-first player look utterly selfish—more selfish, by the way, than Johnson had ever looked.

Battista had requested Chrebet for a story of a different angle, and it was he who offered up his controversial words on Hackett unsolicited but on the record. Chrebet, of course, backtracked once he felt the heat within the organization and blamed Battista for burning him.

With that, Chrebet had found yet another self-manufactured reason to boycott reporters while hiding in the trainer's room or weight room or wherever else during the 45 minutes per day that reporters have access to the locker room.

Chrebet, once a darling in the organization, a story thought too good to be true, had suddenly alienated the very group of reporters and columnists who had helped build his sterling persona and image to what it had become, surely helping him make a lot of money along the way.

He'd so put off reporters and made it so difficult for them to work with him that there were suggestions amongst the beat writers when he was signed to a new contract on the eve of the 2003 season that the press boycott the formal press conference the team was

conducting at the Downtown Marriott Hotel announce the deal.

That, the reporters figured, would have been fitting message for Chrebet as he sat at the podiu table with his wife, their infant son, his parents, an agent for their special moment staring at an emp ballroom with no reporters to ask him questions abou the millions he'd just been signed for.

The only thing that kept the reporters fron carrying out that plan was respect for the team's vic president in charge of public relations, Ron Colangelo Colangelo was the person organizing the pres conference for the team and no one wanted to sabotage his press conference and make him look bad when it was Chrebet who was the root of the problem.

Either the batteries ran out or the bulbs burnt out from Tampa Bay to New Jersey, because the Jets failed to find their way out of the day and were waxed by the Steelers 20-3.

A CHANGED CHREBET

Once Keyshawn Johnson was out of his hair and Wayne Chrebet was more established on the team, a different side of him began to surface.

In 2001, with the Jets' offense struggling and Chrebet out of the lineup with an injury, he watched a Jets road loss from his New Jersey home with his wife and some of her friends. A couple days after the game, Chrebet, clearly taking a shot at offensive coordinator Paul Hackett's conservative offense, said that his wife and her friends were calling out what running play the Jets were going to run before it would unfold before their eyes on the TV set.

When reporters wrote about Chrebet's account of the incident, Chrebet realized the heat he'd created inside the organization and, of course, blamed the messengers. That began a boycott of reporters by Chrebet, who blamed them with the age-old player excuse, taking his comments out of context and blowing the situation out of proportion.

In the 2002 season, Chrebet was at it again, seemingly creating a media frenzy and then going into hiding.

Chrebet, by his own volition and not being provoked by a reporter's questions, lashed out at

Hackett in a *New York Times* story, telling the reporter, Judy Battista, that he and Hackett had no relationship whatsoever and strongly indicating that Hackett was simply ignoring him in the offense. Oh, and by the way, Chrebet's comments came with the team in the midst of a three-game winning streak, making the supposed underdog team-first player look utterly selfish—more selfish, by the way, than Johnson had ever looked.

Battista had requested Chrebet for a story of a different angle, and it was he who offered up his controversial words on Hackett unsolicited but on the record. Chrebet, of course, backtracked once he felt the heat within the organization and blamed Battista for burning him.

With that, Chrebet had found yet another self-manufactured reason to boycott reporters while hiding in the trainer's room or weight room or wherever else during the 45 minutes per day that reporters have access to the locker room.

Chrebet, once a darling in the organization, a story thought too good to be true, had suddenly alienated the very group of reporters and columnists who had helped build his sterling persona and image to what it had become, surely helping him make a lot of money along the way.

He'd so put off reporters and made it so difficult for them to work with him that there were suggestions amongst the beat writers when he was signed to a new contract on the eve of the 2003 season that the press boycott the formal press conference the team was conducting at the Downtown Marriott Hotel to announce the deal.

That, the reporters figured, would have been a fitting message for Chrebet as he sat at the podium table with his wife, their infant son, his parents, and agent for their special moment staring at an empty ballroom with no reporters to ask him questions about the millions he'd just been signed for.

The only thing that kept the reporters from carrying out that plan was respect for the team's vice president in charge of public relations, Ron Colangelo. Colangelo was the person organizing the press conference for the team and no one wanted to sabotage his press conference and make him look bad when it was Chrebet who was the root of the problem.